PRAISE FOR
Gaza Faces History

"Enzo Traverso delivers a stinging riposte, rigorously anchored in his mastery of European Jewish history, to the virtually unanimous sanctification by Western elites of Israel's genocidal war on Gaza, and their dishonest weaponization of anti-Semitism (in some cases by true anti-Semites on the far right) to attack supporters of Palestinian rights."

—Rashid Khalidi,
author of *The Hundred Years' War on Palestine*

"In the face of a massive attempt at distortion of facts comes this lucid analysis that explains, among other things, why the West is unable and unwilling to stop arming Israel, how the memory of the Holocaust is utilized in the defense of Israel, and how Israel succeeds in posing as the victim while destroying Gaza under a hail of bombs and much, much more."

—Raja Shehadeh,
author of *We Could Have Been Friends, My Father and I* and *What Does Israel Fear from Palestine?*

"One of the world's leading exemplars of the virtues of thinking with history, Enzo Traverso offers a uniquely important voice of critique: his latest intervention, impassioned and searching, could not be more timely."

—Mark Mazower,
author of *Dark Continent: Europe's Twentieth Century*

"In this somber and eloquent book, Enzo Traverso situates the atrocities of October 7, and Israel's destruction of Gaza, in a historical sequence that encompasses both the Shoah and the Nakba, the crimes of Nazism and the crimes of colonization. The result is a work of erudition and moral gravitas, offering a devastating indictment of the rhetorical subterfuge by which Israel and its supporters in the West have justified Gaza's slaughter."

—Adam Shatz,
author of *The Rebel's Clinic:
The Revolutionary Lives of Frantz Fanon*

"Hard-hitting and urgent, *Gaza Faces History* blends political acumen and historical insight to offer a critical account of the public debates that have taken place since October 7, 2023. Traverso's 'contrapuntal' approach challenges the common sense around questions of anti-Semitism and anti-Zionism, victims and perpetrators, and political violence. Without minimizing the complexities of the crisis in which we find ourselves, the book concludes with a necessary binational vision—the only way forward."

—Michael Rothberg,
author of *The Implicated Subject:*
Beyond Victims and Perpetrators

"This wide-ranging essay by master historian Enzo Traverso presents a courageously unsparing analysis of the debate about Gaza. Ranging from the tension between universalism and orientalism in the West, the role of national myths and appropriate historical analogies, to the efficacy of anticolonial and revolutionary violence, *Gaza Faces History* challenges the shibboleths that distort understanding of conflict in the land between the river and the sea. It will, I suspect, make for difficult, if necessary, reading for some."

—A. Dirk Moses,
author of *The Problems of Genocide*

"In this edifying little work, Enzo Traverso reflects on Israel's war on Gaza in light of his experience as historian and intellectual. He thus offers the reader a condensed overview of decades of research and thinking on closely related issues, providing a much deeper perspective on the Gaza tragedy."

—Gilbert Achcar,
author of *The Arabs and the Holocaust:*
The Arab-Israeli War of Narratives

Gaza
Faces
History

**Also by
Enzo Traverso**

Gaza
Faces
History

Enzo
Traverso

Translated from
the French by
Willard Wood

Other Press
New York

Originally published in Italian as *Gaza davanti alla storia* in 2024 by
Editori Laterza, Rome
Copyright © Enzo Traverso, 2024
Translation copyright © Willard Wood, 2024

Production editor: Yvonne E. Cárdenas
Text designer: Patrice Sheridan
This book was typeset in Minion Pro and DIN Pro by
Alpha Design & Composition of Pittsfield, NH

10 9 8 7 6 5 4 3 2 1

Hardcover ISBN 978-1-63542-554-3
E-book ISBN 978-1-63542-555-0

Library of Congress Control Number: 2024942160

Contents

Enemies might triumph over Gaza (the storming sea might
triumph over an island…they might chop down all
its trees).
They might break its bones.
They might implant tanks on the insides of its children and
women. They might throw it into the sea, sand, or blood.
But it will not repeat lies and say "Yes" to invaders.
It will continue to explode.
It is neither death, nor suicide. It is Gaza's way of
declaring that it deserves to live.

—MAHMOUD DARWISH, FROM "SILENCE FOR GAZA," (1973),
TRANSLATED BY SINAN ANTOON

Preface

This brief essay is set against the tragic backdrop of the war in Gaza and the heated controversy that ensued. The Hamas attack of October 7, 2023, was met almost everywhere with condemnation, as was necessary and understandable. On the other hand, the murderous, devastating fury that Israel unleashed in the succeeding months has elicited a much more temperate response. Some, embarrassed but indulgent, have taken issue, generally in benevolent tones. The rare critics who have spoken against Israel's policy have been careful to confirm their underlying sympathy and solidarity. The subtext of these editorials has almost always been the same: "Frankly, you've gone overboard, and we can't help criticizing your brutal methods, but we're doing so because we're on your side, as always, and want to help you fight the monsters on the other side." The countries of what is now called the Global South have expressed their unanimous outrage at the destruction of Gaza, whereas the West—that is, the great majority of its governments and media—has approved or even facilitated it, widening the gap between Western elites and public opinion.

The following pages grew out of this observation. The text was not written, therefore, with serene detachment. Rather, it is an attempt to elaborate on a first line of thought, making no attempt to hide the feelings of astonishment, disbelief, discouragement, and anger that washed over me in recent months. I might say, paraphrasing Sartre, that this is a text written *in situation*. No one should be misled by the title, *Gaza Faces History*. I am not a specialist on the Middle East, nor on the Arab-Israeli conflict, nor on Palestine. I don't pretend to analyze the war or describe its players, different perspectives, or geopolitical dimension. Others already do that much better than I, with tools and knowledge that I don't possess. My objective in these pages is different. I have wanted to take a critical look at the political and intellectual debate that the Gaza crisis has stirred up, trying to untangle its knotted skeins of history and memory. In short, it is a critical meditation on the present and the ways that history has been summoned to interpret it. The topic is vast and deserves a more exhaustive study than these hastily written notes, but an emergency exists. A historian may at times deviate from his usual habits and take risks, particularly if he has no illusions about practicing a science free from value judgments—and I do not.

It is clear to all that this war marks an inflection point, not only for its geopolitical consequences but also for how Palestinians and Israelis are seen by the rest of the world. Of course, the war is happening in the present, and we are not yet in a position to write its history. The historicization of great events takes time, as well as established and accessible sources, a long view, and, indispensably, critical distance. At some future point, the Gaza war will undoubtedly find its historians. For now, we can only take stock of the public use being made of the past, and reflect on what history gives us in the way of tools to examine the present, and the questionable, sometimes unworthy, ways history is used. That has been my main interest here. My point of view is dissonant, in the sense that it does not coincide with the axioms of that small portion of the world known as the West, which claims to have a monopoly on power as well as on morality. To this chorus of consensus, my text will act as a "counterpoint," on the invitation that Edward Said made to intellectuals years ago, deploring that their voices were heard less and less, drowned out in the growing roar of the media. Yet when we change our point of observation and put ourselves in the position of those who are experiencing this war, the dissonant voices say quite obvious things.

The present text started as an article in the Italian daily *Il Manifesto* last December, reprinted in an updated English-language version in *Jacobin*; also, from an interview given to the French newspaper *Mediapart*, which was subsequently translated into several languages. The reactions these efforts received encouraged me to write a longer essay, clarifying some of my earlier ideas.

I am grateful to Willard Wood for his elegant translation and to Judith Gurewich for her thoughtful comments and suggestions. I am touched by the enthusiasm with which she agreed to publish the essay at Other Press, in the firm belief that, beyond the different points of view one may have on so delicate and controversial a topic, a critical voice deserves to be heard.

Ithaca, New York, July 10, 2024

Gaza
Faces
History

1

Perpetrators and Victims

In a remarkable essay on the aerial bombardments during World War II, the German novelist W. G. Sebald seeks out the reasons for the silence that, at the end of the conflict, surrounded the suffering endured by his fellow citizens.[1] In 1945, Germany had been devastated. Close to 600,000 of its citizens had died under the rubble of its annihilated cities, an even greater number of civilians had been injured, and several million had been forced into homelessness and displacement. Yet this extreme suffering was left unspoken and quietly internalized by the population; hardly anyone dared to discuss it openly. True, occupied Germany was no longer a sovereign nation, but the silence had deeper causes. The Germans knew that, even as bombs and firestorms were consuming their cities, the Wehrmacht, the police, and the SS were perpetrating crimes far more serious than those they themselves had suffered. This would explain the guilty silence they adopted and their single-minded efforts to clear away the ruins and rebuild their cities in the postwar period.

The suffering inflicted on German civilians during and after World War II, when millions were expelled from Central Europe, is indisputable. Yet when Martin Heidegger referred to it, to reverse the roles and present Germany as the victim of external aggression, Herbert Marcuse put an end to their correspondence. Such a position put Heidegger "outside of Logos," he wrote, "outside of the dimension in which a conversation between men is even possible."[2] Only in the late 1990s, once a reunified Germany had fully incorporated the memory of Nazi crimes into its historical conscience, was it possible for the country's own suffering during World War II to be studied, acknowledged, and debated in the public sphere without provoking animosity or seeming apologetic or self-serving.[3] In this sense, I have the impression that the great majority of our columnists and commentators have become "Heideggerians," tending to substitute the aggressors for the victims, except that today's aggressors are no longer the vanquished but the victors.

The war in Gaza is not World War II, that much is clear, but historical analogies—which are not homologies—can guide us, even if their actors are different and their events on differing scales. Thus it was that, in 1994, French historian Jean-Pierre Chrétien spoke of the genocide against the Tutsi as "tropical Nazism," and that the term "genocide" resurfaced in Europe during the war in former Yugoslavia, notably after the massacre in Srebrenica.[4] With genocide, however complex its historical context, there is always a perpetrator and a victim. And tomorrow's writer who recounts the war in Gaza will have to part with Sebald's assessment, because today the roles are reversed. While Israel destroys Gaza under a hail of bombs, Israel is presented as the victim of "the greatest pogrom in history after the Holocaust."

The situation is paradoxical—a Nuremberg trial where it's not the Nazis' atrocities that face judgment but those committed by the Allies. The Nuremberg trials, which have come to symbolize the victor's justice, were riddled with contradictions—the Allied war crimes were ignored or even, as in the famous case of the Katyn massacre, attributed to the Nazis—but no one has seriously disputed the defendants' guilt.[5] Since October 7, on the other hand, Israel has posed as a victim. The destruction of Gaza? A deplorable excess in a legitimate war of self-defense, the overreaction of a nation under threat, protecting itself by all available means. In the 1980s, the conservative historian Ernst Nolte characterized the Nazi crimes as "reactive." While certainly regrettable, they were a response to the very real threat of Bolshevism, the "logical and factual prius," or precondition, of the to-talitarianisms of the twentieth century and the war on the Eastern front.[6] Today the "logical and factual prius" is called Hamas, a movement whose sole raison d'être is hatred of Israel.

In the twilight years of the Cold War, during the *Historikerstreit*, the heated debates on the analogy between Nazi atrocities and those of the Stalinist regime, conservatives all defended Nolte, who had courageously brought Hitler's motives to light. The fact that the Führer's worldview was based on a radical anti-Bolshevism surely counted as an attenuating circumstance. Nazi crimes had to be put in perspective. The newspapers that defended Nolte at the time, chief among them the *Frankfurter Allgemeine Zeitung*, are today staunch supporters of Israel.[7] In their view, Islamic fundamentalism, with which they identify Palestine, threatens the West today just as Communism did in the last century. The ideological motivations of the pro-Israeli front, so intransigent in the fight against anti-Semitism, are fundamentally the same as those that, forty years ago, prompted Germany's leading conservative daily to take an indulgent stance toward Nolte's apologia of Nazism. In both cases, the roles had been reversed: in the debates of the time, the victims were the Germans, not the Jews; today, the victims are the Israelis, not the Palestinians.

The dominant discourse around October 7 turns this date into a kind of negative epiphany, a sudden appearance of evil that triggered a war of reparation. On that day, the counter was reset to zero, as though its events were the sole cause of the tragedy. October 7 tore the veil from Hamas and Israel, assigning each its role, as perpetrator and victim. The Gaza Strip, a territory of 2.4 million people, subjected to total segregation for the past seventeen years, has thus become a cradle of evil, where unscrupulous murderers act with impunity, turning civilians into "human shields." The reality is that the destruction of Gaza is the culmination of a long process of oppression and eradication. Twenty-two years ago, in August 2002, Edward Said described Israeli violence during the Second Intifada in these terms:

> Gaza is surrounded by an electrified wire fence on three sides; imprisoned like animals, Gazans are unable to move, unable to work, unable to sell their vegetables or fruit, unable to go to school. They are exposed from the air to Israeli planes and helicopters and are gunned down like turkeys on the ground by tanks and machine guns. Impoverished and starved, Gaza is like a human nightmare [...] involv[ing] thousands of soldiers in the humiliation, punishment, and intolerable

enfeeblement of each Palestinian, without regard
for age, gender, or illness. Medical supplies are
held up at the border, ambulances are fired upon
or detained. Hundreds of houses are demolished,
and hundreds of thousands of trees and agricul-
tural land are destroyed in acts of systematic
collective punishment against civilians, most of
whom are already refugees from Israel's destruction of their society in 1948.[8]

October 7 was not a sudden explosion of hate; it
had a long genealogy. It was a tragedy methodically
prepared by those who would now like to be seen as
the victims. The tragedy is still unfolding, which is all
the more reason not to reverse the roles. A quick look
at the chronology will allow us to understand how the
October 7 "pogrom" came about. Since Israel's with-
drawal in 2005, the Gaza Strip has endured several attacks from the Israel Defense Forces (IDF) that have
left thousands of dead in their wake: 1,400 Palestinians in 2008 (as against thirteen Israelis); 170 in 2012;
and 2,200 in 2014. On March 30, 2018, a large peaceful
demonstration against the blockade of Gaza ended in a
massacre: 189 dead and 6,000 wounded. In 2023, from
January 1 to October 6, the IDF had already killed 248
Palestinians in the occupied territories and arrested
another 5,200. Between 2008 and October 6, 2023, the

IDF killed almost 6,400 Palestinians, including over 5,000 Gazans, and wounded 158,440, while Israeli casualties from Hamas and other Islamist groups came to 310 dead and 6,460 wounded.[9] There are about 1.5 million Palestinian refugees in Gaza, more than half the population. The unemployment rate is 50 percent, and 80 percent of the population lives below the poverty line. GDP has fallen steadily in recent years, making the humanitarian intervention of the United Nations Relief and Works Agency for Palestine Refugees in the Near East (UNRWA) a condition of survival. Those under age twenty-five make up 75 percent of the population, and virtually all of them have lived in segregated conditions since birth. A few miles away, just beyond the electric fence, protected by the Iron Dome, an antimissile shield that intercepts rockets, the Israelis live like Europeans. Tel Aviv is as cosmopolitan, modern, feminist, and gay friendly as Berlin. Its cultural industry exports TV series all over the world, and its gastronomy has recently gained wide acclaim. That's the backdrop for October 7.

The concept of genocide cannot be used lightly; it belongs to the realm of law and, as many researchers have pointed out, is ill-suited to the social sciences. The term has always been used for political ends, to stigmatize enemies and defend historical causes. This is true, and we need to be aware of it, but the concept cannot be ignored, especially now. The only normative definition we have, codified at the United Nations Genocide Convention of 1948, accurately describes the current situation in Palestine. It was on the basis of this definition that the International Court of Justice sounded the alarm about the risk of genocide in the Gaza Strip and called on the international community to take measures to stop it. According to Article II of this convention, genocide occurs whenever "acts [are] committed with intent to destroy, in whole or in part, a national, ethnic, racial or religious group, as such." The intent must imply at least one of these crimes:

a) killing members of the group;
b) causing serious bodily or mental harm to members of the group;
c) deliberately inflicting on the group conditions of life calculated to bring about its physical destruction in whole or in part;
d) imposing measures intended to prevent births within the group.[10]

Clearly this description describes exactly what is happening in Gaza today.

As early as October 15, 2023, eight hundred researchers from different disciplines, including international law and Holocaust and genocide studies, warned of a risk of genocide in Gaza. In subsequent months, the *Journal of Genocide Research* opened a forum on the issue, publishing numerous essays analyzing the implications of the destruction of Gaza for a theory of genocide.[11] For Raz Segal, a professor in Holocaust and genocide studies at Stockton University (New Jersey), Gaza is a "textbook case of genocide."[12] A. Dirk Moses, one of the most reputable scholars in this research field, for whom speaking of genocide is extremely difficult from a purely legalistic point of view, emphasizes that "Israeli politicians and military personnel have made numerous statements with genocidal connotations."[13] He mentions in particular Prime Minister Benjamin Netanyahu, who on October 28 affirmed his intention of annihilating Gaza by quoting the biblical episode of the Jews' implacable war against the Amalekites (the passage, at 1 Samuel 15.3, reads: "Now go and smite Amalek, and utterly destroy all that they have, and spare them not; but slay both man and woman, infant and suckling, ox and sheep, camel and ass").[14]

The historian Omer Bartov has rightly noted that the Genocide Convention, triggered by the Holocaust, "set a very high bar to identifying genocide as only an event of similar scope, ideological clarity, and bureaucratic efficiency." This also, he adds, "created a gap" between the legal definition of genocide, which is fairly broad and open to interpretation, and the popular

image of genocide, which has "to resemble the Holocaust in order to merit that title."[15] Genocides differ in
scale and may be committed using a variety of means.
Extermination can be carried out with bullets, gas
chambers, or machetes; by deporting tens of thousands
of people into the desert or other regions lacking the
means of subsistence, as in Namibia in 1904, or Ana-
tolia in 1916; by inducing famine or by consciously fail-
ing to stop one, as the British did in Bengal in 1943;[16]
or by destroying a town through systematic bombing
planned by artificial intelligence (AI). The extermination of Europe's Jews had several aims, including an
ideological and racial imperative. The aim of colonial
genocides in Africa and Asia was to conquer and sub-
jugate; other genocides, such as that of North America's Indians, aimed at extermination and replacement.

The history of the war in Gaza will be written
in decades to come; today, the massacre needs to be
stopped. That is the function of a warning about genocide in progress. Commentators who interpret this
warning as an anti-Semitic attempt to minimize the
Holocaust or deny its uniqueness are just proving how
shortsighted, out of touch, and dangerous a mystical
and self-referential memory can become.

It might be said that the massacre of the residents
of Gaza follows on the recent massacres in Aleppo and
Mosul, and that its casualty numbers are dwarfed by

those of the air raids that destroyed German, Soviet, and Japanese cities in World War II. True, but those cities were martyred in wars that pitted opponents of comparable size against one another. In Aleppo and Mosul, the fighting advanced block by block, and building by building, as in Stalingrad. The civilians there became hostages from being trapped in a conflict where the belligerents were determined to destroy each other. The concept of war—a term used here in keeping with the usage of recent months—is not entirely appropriate to describe what is happening in Gaza, where there are not two armies facing off. Rather, an enormously powerful and sophisticated war machine is methodically eliminating a set of urban centers inhabited by close to two and a half million people. The destruction is unilateral, continuous, and inexorable. We are not dealing with two armies, given the disparity between the IDF and Hamas, but with executioners and victims, an army and a civilian population—precisely the conditions associated with genocide.

The language now in general use hides a flagrant hypocrisy, on the one hand denying Hamas fighters the status of legitimate adversaries on the pretext that they are a terrorist group, and on the other describing the tens of thousands of Palestinian civilians killed during the methodical razing of Gaza as "collateral damage" or, for the boldest commentators, victims of "war crimes." War crimes, whether intentional or accidental, are not a war's objective; they are one of its consequences. The destruction of Gaza, however, *is* the objective of the Israeli offensive. The most extreme factions of Netanyahu's government have ambitious goals and would like to carry out an ethnic cleansing of the Gaza Strip, expelling its inhabitants across the Egyptian border or out to sea. In January, eleven ministers of the present government took part in a rally of extreme Zionists in favor of recolonizing Gaza.[17]

One of the goals of the 1948 United Nations convention was to overcome the limitations of the Nuremberg trials, where Nazi crimes were treated as war crimes. But genocide cannot be reduced to a war crime. This is why, in its order of January 26, 2024, the United Nations' International Court of Justice recognized that South Africa's accusation of genocide was at least "plausible" and ordered Israel to take all measures in its power to prevent its army from committing acts of genocide in the Gaza Strip. Over the following months, the situation worsened, and the court issued a second order to alleviate the famine that had now "settled in" across the ravaged territory. Israel ignored these orders and continued its murderous campaign; its allies did nothing to stop it. On May 20, the prosecutor of the International Criminal Court asked that an arrest warrant be issued for Benjamin Netanyahu and his defense minister, Yoav Gallant. Western heads of state, starting with President Joe Biden, expressed outrage. The International Criminal Court is the direct descendant of the Nuremburg courts; its initiatives are praised as long as they target the West's enemies, such as Russia or Serbia, or the barbarians of the Global South, such as the butchers of Kigali; they provoke an outcry when they are directed at Israeli leaders.

2 | Orientalism

It's a commonplace to describe the State of Israel as a democratic island in a sea of obscurantism, and Hamas as a horde of bloodthirsty beasts—echoes of the nineteenth century, when the West perpetrated genocide in the name of its civilizing mission. In the global world of the twenty-first century, Orientalism is not dead; it saturates the atmosphere. Its basic postulates remain unchanged, fixed in an imaginary dichotomy between civilization and barbarism, progress and backwardness, enlightenment and darkness.[1] The West, as Edward Said observed in his seminal essay of more than forty years ago, is able to define itself only in opposition to a radical otherness, that of a colonial, nonwhite humanity considered to be of lesser value and hierarchically inferior.[2] The difference between the era analyzed by Said in *Orientalism* and today lies in the fact that in the nineteenth century, the conquering

West claimed to be spreading its enlightenment, whereas today it sees itself as a besieged fortress.

It is generally agreed that having been wounded by the "barbaric" Hamas attack, Israel, "the only democracy in the Middle East," has the right to defend itself: all our heads of state have made the pilgrimage to Tel Aviv to assure Netanyahu of their support. And this support has been unwavering, even after the U.N. Security Council's resolution for a ceasefire in Gaza— which will remain wishful thinking until someone steps up to enforce it—even after the U.N.'s International Court of Justice recognized that there was a risk of genocide, and even after the International Criminal Court's prosecutor requested arrest warrants for Netanyahu and his defense chief Gallant for "crimes against humanity" and the "crime of extermination." President Biden called this legal action "outrageous." Alongside ritual declarations of Israel's right to self-defense, no one ever mentions the Palestinians' right to resist a decades-long aggression, because no one recognizes that the Palestinians have a history.

The theme of civilization's struggle against barbarism, now explicitly reformulated as a duel between Western democracy and Islamic terrorism, has found its most cynical expression in the words of some IDF spokesmen quoted in the Israeli media, notably in *+972* and *Local Call*. The barbarians of Hamas, they say, kill civilians and fire rockets blindly at Israeli towns, hoping that some will evade interception and cause damage. The IDF, on the other hand, personifies technological progress: its bombs are not blind but choose their targets with the help of AI. According to a former intelligence officer, the Israeli army has developed a program called *Habsora* (The Gospel) that generates its targets automatically and functions as "a mass assassination factory." As another IDF officer explains, "Nothing happens by accident. When a 3-year-old girl is killed in a home in Gaza, it's because someone in the army decided it wasn't a big deal for her to be killed—that it was a price worth paying to hit [another] target. We are not Hamas. These are not random rockets. Everything is intentional. We know exactly how much collateral damage there is in every home."[3]

The investigations that followed the killing of seven humanitarian aid workers on April 1 uncovered the existence of a second line of AI programs, known as Lavender, for marking targets and generating kill lists. It identified 37,000 low-level Hamas operatives, noncombatants, who were candidates for air strikes using "dumb bombs" (as opposed to "smart bombs," which are supposedly capable of surgical strikes but are more expensive). That day, the algorithms, which are not programmed to distinguish the value of human life according to race or religion, triggered dumb bomb strikes against Australian, British, and Polish aid workers. This was a tragic mistake; they had been killed with bombs reserved for Palestinians. As an officer explained about the bombs' usefulness, "You don't want to waste expensive bombs on unimportant people."[4]

It would be hard to find a better example than this of "instrumental rationality," a calculating reason unhampered by any human or social considerations, which Max Weber, followed by Theodor W. Adorno and Max Horkheimer, identified as the mainspring of Western civilization.[5] After October 7, the acceptable threshold for collateral damage rose considerably, and the number of children killed by bombs has climbed into the thousands. To date, Hamas has "barbarically" killed close to 1,200 Israelis, including 800 civilians; the IDF has "intelligently" killed 40,000 Palestinians, of whom perhaps a quarter were Hamas combatants. Many analysts estimate that a further 20,000 dead lie under the rubble.

Everything is planned: the destruction of roads, buildings, schools, hospitals, universities, museums, monuments, and even cemeteries, flattened by bulldozers; interruptions in the supply of water, electricity, natural gas, gasoline, and Internet service; the denial of access to food and medical supplies; the evacuation of more than 1.8 million of the 2.3 million Gazans toward the southern portion of the Strip, where they are bombed and displaced again; disease, epidemics, and now famine. Unable to eradicate Hamas, the IDF has set about eliminating the Palestinian intelligentsia: academics, doctors, technicians, journalists, artists, intellectuals, and poets. The warning issued by the U.N.'s International Court of Justice is not abstract: the Palestinian population of Gaza, uprooted and deprived of the most elementary conditions of survival, is the target of a planned and relentless massacre. To repeat, Israel's war against Gaza has all the hallmarks of genocide. But nothing can be done. The word *genocide* has been banned by the media, who, when absolutely forced to use it, enclose it in quotation marks and produce a supposedly objective scholar—an "expert"—to qualify the accusation or simply deny it altogether. We have reached the core of the "dialectic of Enlightenment": the International Court of Justice is indeed the legal expression of a universal idea of humanity inherited from the Enlightenment, but its principles clash with Orientalist prejudices, which limit its scope to within the borders of the West, the cradle of civilization. The law affirms universal principles, but the great powers want that legal theory enframed within their system of domination. In its origins, international law was conceived as a "European public law" (*jus publicum europeum*), whose norms were valid only within the Old World.

Colonial conquests fell outside its jurisdiction, and its principles did not apply to colonized peoples. Today, the International Court of Justice has warned of the risk of genocide in Gaza, after the case was brought to it by South Africa. Meanwhile, the request made to the International Criminal Court to arrest Benjamin Netanyahu and his minister of defense for crimes against humanity came from a British prosecutor of Pakistani descent. This southward shift of international humanitarian law has major symbolic import. Universalism has always been about the West extending its values to the whole planet; its own nations had no lessons to learn. The peoples of the Global South might receive humanitarian aid from the West but not administer international law. It is this symbolic shift—both cultural and political—that the Western heads of state ultimately find "outrageous" and intolerable.

At the height of Orientalism, at the turn of the twentieth century, Jews were part of the West but played the role of unwanted guests, excluded and despised. Even the most powerful among them—Gerson von Bleichröder, Bismarck's banker, and Walther Rathenau, the Weimar Republic's minister of foreign affairs, for example—were stigmatized and regarded as vulgar upstarts.[6] Their thinking, as Edward Said noted, marked a *contrappunto* to the dominant discourse. Today, Jews have been "whitewashed" and are at home within so-called Judeo-Christian civilization. Not only are they an integral part of the West, they have become its symbol. They are loved and adulated by those who once despised and persecuted them. In Western Europe, the fight against anti-Semitism has become the flag behind which all postfascist and far-right movements rally, ready to fight "Islamic barbarism," before they have even shed the rags of their former anti-Semitism.

In 1949, after visiting what remained of the Warsaw ghetto, W. E. B. Du Bois came to the conclusion that racism was not limited to the "color line." The phenomenon was more complex, as the genocide of the Jews proved.[7] Racial hatred also existed within white Europe and could take radical form: by the end of the nineteenth century, it had spread to religious divisions, and during World War II it would be transformed into a policy of extermination. But now that the Jews have crossed over to the right side, Netanyahu seems determined to reestablish the demarcation. The peculiar alliance between Israel's Jewish supremacists and the white supremacists in the United States, who are among the most ardent defenders of the settlement of the West Bank,[8] as well as the embraces between the hawks of the pro-Israeli right and the leaders of the right-wing Rassemblement National (National Rally) party in France's National Assembly, are eloquent demonstrations of the same phenomenon. The paradox lies in the predominance of this imaginary color line in a mixed-race and "hybridized" global world, where WASPs (white Anglo-Saxon Protestants) are now a minority in the United States; European countries (including former centers of emigration like Italy) have become multiethnic; and Oriental Jews (Mizrahim) from the Maghreb and the Middle East make up half of the Israeli population. The "color line" is a mental and political construct that doesn't care about reality. Israelis belong to the West regardless of their ethnic origins.

In the United States, during the first half of the twentieth century, it was difficult to classify Jews in society. Neither Black nor entirely white, they blurred existing social divisions and did not belong squarely on either side of the color line. Nicole Lapierre has devoted some illuminating pages to the phenomenon of "black mimesis," made famous in mass culture by *The Jazz Singer*, the first talkie film, directed in 1927 by Alan Crosland, produced by Warner Bros., and starring Al Jolson (aka Asa Yoelson, of Lithuanian Jewish origin). The film is in the minstrel show tradition, which was extremely popular at the turn of the twentieth century: white entertainers, disguised as Blacks, performed a repertoire of African American music and dance. Popular with Jewish actors starting in the late nineteenth century, this comic genre has been interpreted both as an expression of the racial stereotypes of the period and as revealing a Judeo-Black affinity based on the identification of one oppressed minority with another.

Blackface, Lapierre suggests, was instrumental in Americanizing Jewish immigrants: by blackening their faces, Jews made themselves whiter. Conforming to the racial divisions of American society and reenacting the dominant racial stereotypes allowed them to enter the white world. At a time when Jews were subject to discrimination and anti-Semitism, minstrel shows helped put them on the right side of the color line, among whites. Also, this mimetic process of putting oneself in the skin of the other gave rise to the Judeo-Black cultural transfers of the twentieth century. The solidarity that grew from it was most strongly expressed in the role that Jews played in the anti-segregation and civil rights movement of Black Americans in the 1950s and 1960s.[9] This was the peculiar dialectics between the Americanization of the Jews, who were gradually accepted within a racially hierarchical society, and the political engagements inherited from their past as an oppressed minority.

Throughout its history, Zionism—which arose as a Jewish "mimesis" of European nationalism—has tried to stamp out other successful forms of mimesis, assimilation, and cultural integration. In Israel, transposing

the color line was carefully accomplished through a
set of educational and cultural policies, with the indis-
pensable support of the media. Oxford historian Avi
Shlaim, in a fascinating autobiography, has retraced his
break with his native land and culture, and the indoc-
trination he underwent in Israel to the point that he
grew disillusioned, emigrated to the United Kingdom,
and became an active anti-Zionist. Born in Baghdad,
he witnessed the disappearance of a Jewish community
that had subsisted in the Middle East for thousands
of years, creating fruitful forms of cultural symbiosis
with the Muslim majority. The history of this community, he believes, can be divided into two parts, with
the watershed in 1950: first the Ottoman Empire and
its successor states, then the birth of Israel, with all
its many consequences for the region. The date marks
a radical break, with two completely different—not
to say opposite—histories on either side. After 1950,
Shlaim observes,

> Arab-Jewish or Mizrahi history becomes part
> of Israel's history and as such divorced from its
> wider regional environment. Zionists are only in-
> terested, obsessively interested, in the first phase
> of Arab-Jewish history; they are profoundly
> uninterested in the second. Interest in the first
> phase is driven not by the search for truth but

by the propaganda need to portray the Jews as
the victims of the endemic Arab persecution, a
portrayal that is then used to justify Israel's own
atrocious treatment of the Palestinians. A rich,
fascinating, and multidimensional history is thus
reduced to the quest for ammunition to use in the
ongoing war against the Palestinians.

This narrative, Shlaim emphasizes, "is not history; it is
the propaganda of the victors."[10]

On arrival in Israel, Jews from Arab countries were
designated as "Orientals," a category that included all
non-Ashkenazim (cataloged in official data under the
heading "Asia/Africa"). Their new identity, Yitzhak
Laor points out, distinguished them from European
Jews, re-creating the traditional colonialist opposition
between East (Islam) and West (Judeo-Christian Europe). The "Orientals" were subjected to an assimilation
process before they could be considered true Israelis.[11]
According to Ilan Halevi, the process required a form
of "mental self-mutilation," comparable in every way to
what Franz Fanon described in the French Antilles.[12]

For Israel's Jewish supremacists and their most ardent supporters, the Christian evangelicals and white
supremacists of the United States and their new allies
on the European far right, the "color line" has been
reestablished. But the recognition goes well beyond

these strands, which are only its most extreme expression. As Gilbert Achcar has pointed out, Jews benefit
today from the "narcissistic compassion" of the West.[13]
It's the same sentiment that prompted *Le Monde*, in
the wake of 9/11, to print the headline "We Are All
Americans"—a phrase it's hard to imagine being applied to the Palestinians. They, however, arouse a spon-
taneous feeling of identification and sympathy among
all of the West's outcasts. In the United States, Black
Lives Matter and other anti-racist movements immediately endorsed the Palestinian cause, sometimes
at the cost of shortcuts that tend to reduce a colonial
issue to its racial dimension. My neighborhood public
swimming pool in Ithaca, New York, which is named
after Alex Haley and mostly used by Black children
and teens, has repainted its facade in the colors of the
Palestinian flag. The Palestinian cause has become the
cause of the Global South.

This brings us to another significant inversion.
The State of Israel was born in 1948 in the exceptional
circumstances of the postwar years. It was the belated
product of a wartime consensus—the alliance between
the Western democracies and the USSR—that was just
starting to fray with the beginning of the Cold War.[14] In
1948, it was Czechoslovakia that supplied the weapons
for the war against the Arab countries. But the egali-
tarian ideal embodied by the kibbutz, where the fact

of having no Arabs made it possible to avoid the colonial exploitation of a native workforce, quickly turned
into a trap and created an inexorable system of exclu-
sion. "To be anticapitalist in Palestine," wrote Hannah
Arendt in 1950, "almost always meant to be practically
anti-Arab."[15] This process was methodically carried
forward over the decades and during Israel's border
wars until it became a system of apartheid. Israel was
not born as "an outpost of imperialism," despite Herzl's
fond wish, as we will see later, but it became one after a
long journey of integration with the West. Netanyahu
is the sinister incarnation of this transformation.

Applying to the history of Zionism the same ana-
lytic criteria that he had earlier applied to European
nationalism, the historian Zeev Sternhell has lucidly
charted Zionism's ingrained debt to Johann Gott-
fried Herder and a "tribalist" ethos. Originating in
Central Europe at the end of the nineteenth century
as a response to the crisis of liberalism and the process of emancipation, Zionism could hardly escape
the cultural constraints of its time. The socialism of its
founding fathers (Berl Katznelson, A. D. Gordon, and
David Ben-Gurion) was an outer, superficial veneer,
underlaid by a robust and far more conventional nationalism.[16] Some Zionist ideologues, including Haim
Arlosoroff and Nachman Syrkin, were openly inspired
by the German nationalism of Oswald Spengler and

Moeller van den Bruck, while Martin Buber, writing
in 1911, indulged in a mystical idealization of Jewish
"blood." This largely suffices to put these intellectuals
alongside Maurice Barrès, Charles Maurras, and Spengler in the anti-Enlightenment camp.[17] Yet Zionism
was looking for a political solution to the problems of
an oppressed people. It came into being as a reaction
to anti-Semitism, which was one of the strands of "the
great battle against the Enlightenment" that would
dominate the twentieth century, but it wanted to combat anti-Semitism with the same weapons and ideas
that were fueling nationalism throughout Europe. As
a Jewish nationalist movement, Zionism almost me-
chanically reproduced all the ideological features of
European nationalism. What distinguished Zionism
was its mythology, which drew on the Bible to claim for
Jews a kind of divine, ancestral right to Palestine. This
initial contradiction would place Zionism somewhere
between a national liberation movement (which is how
Ber Borochov's Marxist Zionist movement Poale Zion
defined itself) and classic settler colonialism. The latter aspect in the end absorbed all others, increasing
the tension. The struggle to find a safe haven turned
into a war to create an exceptionalist state where Jews
would replace the native population, as many European colonialists had already done in North America,
Australia, and South Africa. But Israel was founded in

1948, when the world was entering the era of decolonization, and the Arab world, in Palestine as elsewhere, had
developed a sense of national consciousness. Driven to
create a Jewish national society *without Arabs*, Zionism
always maintained a balance between a secular compo-
nent and a religious. The first was invariably prone to the
excesses of colonial and hierarchical nationalism; the
second—for a long time a minority within the Zionist
movement—laid claim to the land on the basis of biblical myth: if the Jews were the original and legitimate
inhabitants of Palestine, then the Palestinians were only
interlopers. Colonization was in fact a "return," and the
expulsion of the intruders was its necessary precondition.[18] These two forms of colonialism, one secular, the
other religious, have always been inextricably linked at
the heart of Zionism. A. D. Gordon, one of the original
theorists of Labor Zionism, was a nationalist Ukrainian
Jew who settled in Ottoman Palestine in 1904. In his
writings he combined the classic arguments of colonialism (the racial superiority of Europeans over Arabs)
and theology. In 1921 he asked the question "And what
did the Arabs produce in all the years they lived in the
country? Such Jewish creations, or even the creation
of the Bible alone, give us a perpetual right over the
land in which we were so creative, especially since the
people who came after us did not create such works in
this country, or did not create anything at all."[19] Noting

that "The Founders accepted this point of view. This was the ultimate Zionist argument," Sternhell observes that "The centrality of the Bible was responsible both for the importance of historical factors in the thinking of the movement and for the place given to religion and tradition."[20] Today, these two strands, the secular and the religious, have coalesced into a theological-political project that is both radical and redemptive in nature. In consequence, the socialist Zionism of early times has all but disappeared. The Jews were no longer an oppressed nation, and Zionism could not subsist as a national liberation movement.

In 1896, Theodor Herzl, the spiritual father of Israel, published *The Jewish State*, Zionism's founding text, where he presents the future Jewish state as "an outpost of Europe against Asia, the vanguard of civilization against barbarism (*Vorpostendienst der Kultur gegen die Barbarei*)."[21] In 2024, Zionism's ambition remains substantially the same, but Netanyahu is much more respected and listened to than Herzl was over a century ago. Addressing aristocratic elites who considered him an intruder, Herzl insisted that he belonged to the West and begged the European nations for their help. Netanyahu, on the other hand, makes no secret of his arrogance and ingratitude toward them.

Israel has been violating international law for decades, and today its army is destroying Gaza with an arsenal supplied mainly by the United States and, to a much lesser degree, Germany, Italy, and France.[22] The United States could stop the war in a matter of days, but it is unwilling to withdraw its support from a corrupt far-right government run by fundamentalists, racists, and war criminals. It can't, because that very government is an integral part of its geopolitical strategy, and because most Americans feel a narcissistic compassion toward Israelis that they do not feel toward Arabs. The United States has therefore limited itself to recommendations and appeals to moderation, without ever pressuring its ally with the prospect of a cutoff of military and economic aid. While the United States has refused to impose sanctions on a state that has already killed hundreds of doctors, nurses, and humanitarian aid workers, it immediately suspended funding to the UNRWA when the Israeli military published information (never proved) that twelve of the organization's workers (out of 13,000) might have been implicated in the October 7 attack. The United States seems not to care that this double standard excites the indignation of the vast majority of the world.

3

Reason of State

In European Union countries, the memory of the Holocaust is ritually honored as a civil religion celebrating democracy and human rights. Recently it has taken on a different role and been used more and more to defend Israel and fight anti-Zionism, which is now perceived as a form of anti-Semitism. Chancellors Angela Merkel and Olaf Scholz both repeatedly declared that unconditional support of Israel has the force of a "reason of state" (*Staatsräson*) for the Federal Republic of Germany. Starting on October 7, Chancellor Scholz's government, joined by the media, created a witch hunt atmosphere in the country against any form of solidarity with Palestine. Many young Germans found themselves inside a police station for having demonstrated with a Palestinian flag (including several who were citizens of Palestinian descent), to the point that a number of prominent Jews, leaders of major cultural institutions, spoke up in protest.[1] Here again, Germany is only an extreme instance of a broader trend. In the United States, notably, many Jews have also raised their voices to say "Not in my name."

The fact that Merkel and Scholz used a term as ambiguous as "reason of state" is both curious and revealing. The concept is widely understood to refer to a dark and hidden side of power. Usually associated with Machiavelli, though the phrase does not actually appear in his writings—it was forged by Giovanni Botero in 1589—it applies to an unspoken transgression of the law in the name of a higher security imperative. In a state where the death penalty has been abolished, for instance, but the secret service wants to execute a terrorist or other person believed to pose a threat to public order, a reason of state might be invoked. From Machiavelli to Friedrich Meinecke, its theorists, to its less-noble practitioners, e.g., Paul Wolfowitz, all agree that a reason of state denotes the violation by a political power of its own ethical principles in service to a higher interest, generally the safeguarding of its own power—what Machiavelli called "great things" (*grandi cose*)—when it's not just the prince's personal interest. In short, "reason of state" is a term for justifying illegal and immoral actions that are in fact a hidden face of the law. Scholars usually distinguish between "two" Machiavellis: the republican thinker of civic virtue and the cynical advocate of state power, a "teacher of evil," according to a famous sentence of Leo Strauss. The first Machiavelli would be the author of *Discourses on Livy* (1531, written in 1517) and the second the author of *The Prince* (1532, written in 1513). Machiavelli's writings do not escape the destiny of most classics, and they have been the object of multiple controversies. Much more than a systematic theory elaborated by the Florentine political philosopher, Machiavellianism is a creation of his interpreters. The fact remains that the idea of reason of state is commonly described as an immoral form of realpolitik.[2]

The historian of political thought Norberto Bobbio has summed up the concept of reason of state as follows: "By 'reason of state' is meant a set of principles and maxims according to which actions that would be unjustifiable if committed by a single individual are not only justified but at times praised and exalted when performed by the prince or whoever exercises power in the name of the state."[3] The fact that the same action can be considered reprehensible when it is the result of individual behavior and praiseworthy when implemented by the state, Bobbio continues, reveals the gap between politics and morality, paving the way for a so-called political realism that tramples morality to consolidate power. Bobbio develops his argument by citing the seventeenth-century scholar Gabriel Naudé, one of the numerous admirers of Machiavelli. In a famous essay of 1639, Naudé evokes the benefits of the Saint Bartholomew's Day massacre in the light of reasons of state. As with so many "bloody tragedies" that preceded it, the massacre of the French Huguenots was in his view fully justified. While its "barbarism" was undeniable, the massacre was "one of the most necessary and just."[4] Such an apology for wholesale slaughter has no purpose beyond illustrating the theory that the end justifies the means. The same arguments were used by the ideologues of the George W. Bush administration after September 11, 2001, and the invasion of Iraq. Behind the reason of state there is not democracy, there is Guantánamo.

So when the German Republic invokes its own *Staatsraison* to justify its absolute support for Israel, it is implicitly admitting the morally unsavory nature of its policy. We know that Israel is committing crimes, Scholz tells Netanyahu in substance, but these morally reprehensible means are "necessary and just" because they consolidate your power, a goal we unconditionally share. It's for reasons of state, he seems to add, that we tolerate your crimes.

This stance undeniably damages Germany's international reputation and calls into question such fundamental principles of liberal democracy as freedom of speech and open debate in a public forum, with a variety of views. Demonstrations to proclaim solidarity with Palestine have been suppressed, the Palestinian flag censored, numerous activists arrested, and internationally renowned public figures debarred from taking part in conferences against the Israeli war. The silencing of American philosopher Nancy Fraser and the denial of visas to former Greek finance minister Yanis Varoufakis and British surgeon Ghassan Abu-Sittah, who were due to speak at conferences in Cologne and Berlin, are clear evidence of this antidemocratic censorship. Some have noted that Gaza is yet another genocide perpetrated or approved by Germany in little more than a century, from the extermination of the Hereros and Namas in colonial Namibia in the early 1900s to the Jews and Roma/Sinti during World War II. A cruel joke is currently making the rounds, an instance of black humor: "Germany didn't want to miss out: whenever there's a genocide, it's on the side of the executioner!" On November 9 of last year, to mark a fateful day in German history—the anniversary of the collapse of Kaiser Wilhelm's empire (1918), of the pogroms of Kristallnacht in 1938, and of the fall of the Berlin Wall (1989)—the mayor of Berlin decided to project a Star of David with the slogan *Nie wieder ist jetzt!* (Never again is now!) on the Brandenburg Gate. To use the Star of David the same way that swastikas were used during Hitler's era—to adorn the sides of buildings and monuments in German cities—is surprising at the least. This grotesque pastiche of Nazi propaganda, even as Israel was launching its assault on Gaza, shines a troubling light on the unconscious of Germany's leaders.

The policy of unconditional support for Israel does have some advantages for Germany. Above all, it allows Germany to outsource its guilt, while giving it the image of an unwavering foe of anti-Semitism; it situates Berlin's foreign policy squarely in the Western camp,[5] and it marks a new xenophobic development in domestic policy by turning the fight against anti-Semitism into a cudgel to use against immigrants and minorities associated with Islam and to bring them into line. What's wrong with discriminating against immigrants and Muslims, if it's to defend the Jews? There are even conservative representatives in Parliament who would like to require every applicant for a German residence permit to sign a declaration of support for Israel.[6] On June 27, 2024, a new law on naturalization was promulgated, making the recognition of the State of Israel a condition for becoming a citizen. Omer Bartov has recently shown that by interpreting the Holocaust as historically unique, Germany has "put itself in a very dubious moral position," both downplaying its own colonial crimes and "denying Israel's culpability in the ongoing destruction of Gaza, including the murder and starvation of thousands of Palestinian civilians."[7]

Scholars have been discussing for decades the Holocaust's "uniqueness," a concept whose interpretations
are frequently contradictory. For genocide's victims,
their experience is undoubtedly "unique," and a watershed in their lives. Scholars must understand and
respect this feeling, but they know that any historical
event is singular, and that this distinctiveness is relative. Positing an absolute "uniqueness" of the Holocaust is epistemologically sterile (historical events can
be compared), politically irresponsible (crimes can be
repeated; they must be understood, not only commem-
orated), and morally dubious (insofar as it creates a
hierarchy among victims). The German memorial policies are an eloquent illustration of the consequences of
a misleading conception of "uniqueness."[8] Till recent
times, the Holocaust memory was a powerful tool to re-
activate the atonement of other colonial crimes. Today,
the use of the Holocaust to justify Germany's unconditional support for Israel blurs the democratic culture,
education, and memory that the Federal Republic of
Germany has built up over several decades, especially
since the *Historikerstreit* and reunification. This policy
casts Berlin's Holocaust Memorial in a sinister light: far
from embodying a tormented historical consciousness
and the virtues of remembrance, the monument now
appears as a glaring symbol of national hypocrisy. To
people who, like me, belong to countries that did not

"work through" their own colonial past and did not elaborate the legacy of their own crimes—in Italy there are no memorials devoted to the Ethiopian genocide of 1935–1936—Germany often looked like a model of virtuous historical responsibility. Today it has become a warning about the dangerous outcomes of a unilateral memory. "Uniqueness" should not be opposed to universalism.

4

False News of the War

In 1921, the historian Marc Bloch wrote an interesting essay on the spread of false news in wartime. He described how, at the beginning of World War I, just after the invasion of Belgium, German newspapers started publishing more and more stories about the extraordinary atrocities being committed by "the Belgians of both sexes," acting "as bloodthirsty beasts." The false news was obviously fabricated, but in the wartime climate it immediately struck people as indisputable truth. "The error," Bloch wrote, "propagates itself, grows, and ultimately survives only on one condition—that it finds a favorable cultural broth in the society where it is spreading. Through it, people unconsciously express all their prejudices, hatreds, fears, all their strong emotions."[1] These rumors, legends, myths, and lies always arise from preexisting collective representations. False news, Bloch said, "is a mirror wherein the 'collective consciousness' contemplates its own features."[2] Myths are performative, he added: "From the moment that it caused blood to be shed, [the false news] was definitively established. Men moved by a blind and brutal but sincere anger set fires and fired shots; this caused them from then on to harbor a perfectly stubborn faith in the existence of 'atrocities' that could alone give their rage an appearance of fairness."

In the weeks that followed the October 7 attack, the Western press published texts reviving memories of the oldest anti-Semitic myths, but turned against the Palestinians. Bloch was right in saying that false news and legends have always "filled the life of humanity." Many historians of the Inquisition and anti-Semitism have studied the mythology of "ritual murder" from the Middle Ages to tsarist Russia, showing among other things that rumors of Jews killing Christian children to use their blood for ritual purposes spread repeatedly before a pogrom broke out. Similarly, after October 7, most Western media—including many reputedly serious newspapers—published false stories of pregnant women disemboweled, dozens of children beheaded, and babies thrown into ovens by Hamas fighters. TV reporters announced in grave, indignant tones that they had seen terrible images of atrocities that they would not broadcast so as to avoid upsetting their viewers. These inventions put out by the Israeli army were immediately accepted as evidence—Joe

Biden, Anthony Blinken, and ministers from European nations repeated them in their speeches—only to be retracted grudgingly a few weeks later. To debunk these horrific fantasies and discover their source, one had to consult Al Jazeera or counterinformation sites. Meanwhile, the mainstream media has been singularly discreet in disavowing these lies, unwilling to disturb the dominant narrative of Hamas barbarism, anti-Semitic hatred, and Israeli victimhood.

Some retractions are more discreet than others. A few years ago, the field of Jewish studies was rocked by a controversy that drew much media attention. At the heart of the polemic was a "scholarly" work entitled *Pasque di sangue* (2007), devoted to the anti-Semitic myth of ritual murder.[3] Its author, Ariel Toaff, is a historian at Bar Ilan University and the son of Rome's former chief rabbi. Rash in his pronouncements and far from rigorous in his treatment of sources, Toaff concluded that the charges brought by the Inquisition were not always untrue. From the twelfth to the sixteenth century in Trentino, Toaff claimed, the Ashkenazim committed ritual crimes on a number of occasions, driven to violate biblical prohibitions by their hatred of Christians. Though hailed enthusiastically by a few conservative Catholic historians, the book drew an avalanche of criticism disputing its conclusions and demolishing its research and analysis. The

Knesset condemned Toaff, and his father disavowed him. Toaff apologized and afterward recalled the book from bookstores (by which time it had already sold out), republishing it a year later with an afterword that qualified his conclusions somewhat. The episode sparked a debate that raged in the Italian press, far beyond the usual precincts of historiography, with echoes in several countries. It's odd all the same that the major newspapers, so eager to welcome articles to discredit the false news of a ritual crime committed in Trentino in 1457, should have acted with such disregard in retracting false news that they themselves had helped to spread a few days earlier concerning Jewish babies thrown into ovens by Islamists. Whereas early-modern anti-Semitic mythology is intolerable, contemporary Islamophobic allegations have become banal: they have been integrated into our zeitgeist and belong to the natural order of things.

5

Anti-Zionism and Anti-Semitism

The press and especially the news channels are constantly warning us that anti-Semitism is everywhere on the rise. They don't point to specific episodes, content instead to denounce an ancient prejudice that in the context of a Middle East crisis is staging a resurgence. No, they describe a gigantic wave of anti-Semitism that has been sweeping across the globe since October 7. Its epicenter is on American college campuses, just as the epicenter of the anti–Vietnam War movement was on college campuses sixty years ago. *The New York Times* has published a number of articles making the analogy between the current antiwar demonstrations and the earlier ones. The comparison is fair enough, since the United States has not seen protests on this scale since the Vietnam War. Students are well aware of this. In the 1960s, an American army was engaged in war in Southeast Asia; today, Israel is destroying Gaza with weapons supplied by the United States. Like their predecessors, today's students understand that their involvement is crucial to stopping the massacre, that their demonstrations are not mere gestures of solidarity but an uprising organically linked to the Palestinian resistance. In both cases, these movements have been violently denounced, and even repressed. During the Vietnam War, students who occupied college campuses and burned the American flag were painted as being enemies of the free world, communists, and totalitarians. Today they would be branded as anti-Semites.

The accusation is as serious as it is false. When I join pro-Palestinian demonstrations on the Cornell University campus, I see many Jewish students, often waving signs of endorsement from their organizations. At the rallies, Jewish students and professors— sometimes also Israeli students—express their anger at the massacre in Gaza. United in their demand for justice and equality, Jews and Palestinians display brotherly feelings toward each other. When I go home and turn on the TV, I am immediately confronted, flipping through the main U.S. and European channels, with a talk show on the anti-Semitism of the antiwar movement. Mike Johnson, speaker of the United States

House of Representatives, appears on every channel. Surrounded by policemen and people holding Israeli flags—not one of them young enough to be a student—Johnson positions himself next to the pro-Palestinian encampment at New York's Columbia University and denounces anti-Semitism. Shortly afterward, I see him again at a press conference, and still later at a ceremony at the Holocaust Memorial Museum. This same man, a member of the Republican Party and an ardent supporter of Donald Trump, has been repeating for three and a half years that Joe Biden stole the election. Should we believe that the students demonstrating for Palestine are deplorable anti-Semites and the attackers of the Capitol building on January 6, 2021, true defenders of democracy? It strikes me that the journalists, special correspondents, and newscasters who tour American campuses, some with entire crews of photographers and cameramen, and who then tell us about the anti-Semitism of American students are lying and dishonoring their profession.

The reality is that anti-Semitism has been *weaponized*, to use the current expression. Not the anti-Semitism of yesteryear, which was directed against the Jews, but a new, imaginary anti-Semitism aimed at criminalizing any criticism of Israel. The antiwar movement is very broad and diverse, in the United States as in Europe. Within this large constellation, three main clusters stand out quite clearly. The first consists of young people of postcolonial origin, born in Europe or the Americas into families originally from Africa or Asia. For them, the Palestinian cause is a new stage in the struggle against colonialism. Next come African Americans, who identify the liberation of Palestine with a global fight against racism and inequality. Palestinian lives matter. Israel has relegated Palestinians to an apartheid system comparable to what once existed in South Africa. And finally, there are those who are reactivating a specifically Jewish universalist and internationalist tradition, though one that has always stood apart from Zionism—when not opposing it outright. Many of these youths are "non-Jewish Jews," in the sense that Isaac Deutscher gave that term: "heretics" who take part in the Jewish tradition by transcending Judaism.[1] Others are what we might call "Dreyfusards," Jews who will not stand for discrimination, oppression, or killing to be carried out in their name, just as there were French citizens who, believing in a republican ideal of equality and justice, supported the Algerian cause.[2] In the twentieth century, this tradition placed Jews in the vanguard of liberation movements. Clearly, the tradition is still very much alive, and we should be thankful. The media campaign denouncing the alleged anti-Semitism of students who rally in support of Palestine is a direct attack on these three groups. Equating anti-Zionism with anti-Semitism kills three birds with one stone, striking at anti-colonialism, anti-racism, and Jewish nonconformism.

The link between anti-Zionism and anti-Semitism has always been ambiguous. On the one hand, a Jewish nationalist movement was always going to be viewed with hostility by European nationalists who found in anti-Semitism one of their baseline elements. On the other hand, Zionism sought from the outset to use anti-Semitism to achieve its own ends. Anti-Semites wanted to drive out Jews, and Zionists wanted to persuade Jews to emigrate to Palestine—there was ample room for a meeting of minds. The most striking case of convergence between these declared enemies is to be found in the 1933 Haavara Agreements, whose signatories were the Nazi government, a British bank, and the Zionist Federation of Germany, all of whom supported Jewish emigration to Palestine and set about establishing the practical framework (taxation, asset transfers, et cetera).[3] The agreement collapsed after a few years: first, because the Nazis wanted to get rid of the Jews but didn't want a Jewish state; and second, because this agreement clearly had little appeal for those who were opposed to anti-Semitism and working toward an economic boycott of the Third Reich. Whereas anti-fascists tried to create a mass movement against Nazism, Zionists made an agreement with Hitler. These strategies could not coexist without tensions. In the eyes of many anti-fascists, Zionism wished to find a compromise with the Nazis instead of fighting them.

There is no question that, especially on the right, many anti-Zionists were anti-Semitic. Moreover, after the birth of Israel, the Arab world imported many anti-Semitic stereotypes from Europe, which became widespread just as they were waning in their countries of origin. But it's also true that Zionism has always been criticized, and often vehemently rejected, by a large part of the Jewish world. A list of anti-Zionist Jewish intellectuals would fill several volumes. Zionism was one of the many offshoots of the secularization and modernization that transformed the Jewish world starting in the nineteenth century, but for a long time it had relatively few adherents. Today the situation has changed, because Israel is a state, and in a secular world the memory of the Holocaust and the existence of Israel mark out the landscape in which the identity of diasporic Jews is defined.[4] But the situation has also changed because the conservative right and even the extreme far right have become ardent defenders of Zionism, having decided that Arab and Muslim immigrants make far better scapegoats than Jews. Yesterday's anti-Semites are today leading the fight against anti-Zionism, which they denounce as a form of anti-Semitism. Italy offers a paradigmatic example: by their attack on anti-Zionism, the "postfascists," who are in power today and are the legitimate heirs of the racist laws of 1938, can simultaneously affirm their support for Israel and their membership in the Western camp, stigmatize the Left, and pursue xenophobic policies toward migrants.

Today, a persistent media campaign portrays pro-Palestinian students as anti-Semites. In some American universities, they are blacklisted or threatened with sanctions for having taken part in protests against the genocide in Gaza. The sacred principle of freedom of speech is suddenly no longer tolerated because it upsets the powerful donors of major universities, now revealed to be corporations first and spaces of freedom only second. The anti-Zionist organization Jewish Voice for Peace was banned on several U.S. campuses. In Italy, demonstrations in support of Palestine have been brutally shut down (to the point that President Sergio Mattarella, marking a split with the Meloni government, issued a reminder that the people have a right to demonstrate). In Paris, the mayor's office canceled a rally by several anti-racist associations, among them Tsedek, a Jewish anti-Zionist movement, at which the American Jewish philosopher Judith Butler was to have spoken. The people in charge of Paris's cultural policy then explained—presumably with downcast eyes and blushing cheeks—that they had wanted to avoid complicity with an anti-Semitic initiative. Gabriel Attal, France's head of government, appeared at the Institut de Science Politique de Paris—uninvited and in flagrant violation of university autonomy—to announce sanctions against pro-Palestinian activists, after a Zionist student had been removed from a lecture hall where she had been photographing the organizers to denounce them on social networks. Although Jewish students and Jewish organizations took an active and highly visible part in the marches and demonstrations against the genocide in Gaza, a false report quickly spread, widely echoed in the media, that some students were being barred from access to campuses "because they were Jewish." In New York, minivans drove around Columbia University bearing photographs of pro-Palestinian students with their names and the tagline "anti-Semite," a sad throwback to the Nazi Germany of 1935 and the era of the Nuremberg Laws, when Jews were paraded through the streets with a sign around their necks saying *Jude*.

"One easily believes what one needs to believe," Marc Bloch observed in his essay quoted earlier.[5] Many examples confirm this. After World War II, communist Resistance fighters who had been deported to Nazi camps denied the existence of the gulags. In France, a number of them testified in court to defend *Les Lettres Nouvelles*, a cultural magazine that actively promoted the lie that the gulags were an anti-communist fantasy.[6] Their guiding myth had the power and simplicity of a syllogism: the USSR is a socialist country, socialism means freedom, ergo there cannot be concentration camps in the USSR. Anyone who said the contrary was a liar; the gulag was a product of American propaganda. A similar denialism is widespread among many today who are convinced that Israel, a nation risen from the ashes of the Holocaust, could never commit genocide. For them, the U.N. reporters who say the opposite are liars and are being manipulated by pernicious anti-Semitic propaganda. Israel is a genuine democracy, and the occupation of the Palestinian territories a necessary measure to counter an existential threat. Or else it's a misstep, an overreaction—the syndrome outlined by Nolte above—from a country that's in danger. Faith often calls for a denial of reality.

Orientalism is the breeding ground for the myths, lies, and fake news that surround this war. Reversing reality, a paradoxical narrative has emerged that makes Israel the victim, not the oppressor: anti-Zionism is merely a form of anti-Semitism; anti-colonialism has finally revealed its anti-Western, fundamentalist, and anti-Semitic roots. The Judeo-Bolshevist plotters of yore have become the Islamic-leftists of today. Over the past few months, this mythology has spread in just the way that false news did during World War I.

So extensive a reversal of reality is bound to have far-reaching consequences we should reflect on. Fighting anti-Semitism will become increasingly difficult given the distortion and misappropriation of the term. The risks from misusing the concept are very real: if you can conduct a genocidal war in the name of fighting anti-Semitism, many good people will start to think it would be better to abandon such a dubious cause altogether. No one will be able to mention the Holocaust without raising suspicions and doubt; many will come to believe that it is a myth invented to defend the interests of Israel and its allies. The remembrance of the Holocaust as a "civil religion"—the ritual consecration of human rights through the memory of the Shoah's victims—will lose all its power to instruct.[7]

Previously, this "civil religion" served as a paradigm for the remembrance of other genocides and crimes against humanity—from the extermination of the Armenians, to military dictatorships in Latin America, to the Holodomor famine in Ukraine, to Bosnia, and to the Tutsi genocide in Rwanda. If this sacred and institutionalized memory serves only to support Israel and attack the defenders of the Palestinian cause on the pretext of anti-Semitism, our moral, political, and epistemological bearings will become unmoored, with devastating consequences. Certain postulates that make up our moral and political conscience—the

distinction between good and evil, oppressor and oppressed, perpetrator and victim—will be undermined.
Our conception of democracy, which is not limited to a
system of laws but is also founded on our culture, memory, and historical heritage, will be weakened. Anti-
Semitism, which every serious contemporary analysis
found to be receding before October 7, will see a spectacular resurgence.[8] That is why, despite the good faith
of many of its participants, the protest against anti-
Semitism in Paris on November 10, 2023—organized
by all the parties supporting the massacre in Gaza, including the far right—not only seemed slightly obscene
but had deeply regressive political effects.

6

Violence, Terrorism, Resistance

Benny Morris, a "revisionist" Israeli historian who has extensively documented the expulsion of the Palestinians during the 1948 war—and subsequently regretted that the ethnic cleansing was not fully carried out—has described the massacres committed in Palestinian villages by the Irgun (Irgun Z'vai Leumi, IZL), the far-right Zionist militia led by Menachem Begin. The most well-known of these massacres occurred on April 9, 1948, at Deir Yassin, not far from Jerusalem, and left more than two hundred dead. It has remained in people's memories not for its military significance but rather, as Morris says, "for the atrocities committed by the IZL and LHI troops," the paramilitary units of Irgun and the Stern Gang. Events unfolded as follows: "Whole families were riddled with bullets and grenade fragments and buried when houses were blown up on top of them; men, women, and children were mowed down as they emerged from houses; individuals were taken aside and shot. At the end of the battle, groups of old men, women, and children were trucked through West Jerusalem's streets in a kind of 'victory parade' and then dumped in (Arab) East Jerusalem."[1]

Some have viewed the atrocities of October 7 as "the worst pogrom in history after the Holocaust," while others have seen them as the product of a long sequence of Israeli violence. Of course, the one does not justify the other: the decades of occupation don't lessen the horror of the massacre of Israeli children, and conversely a history of anti-Semitism can't be invoked in support of genocide in Gaza. These acts of violence, however, occurred in an explosive context. Perpetrating carnage at a rave party is unquestionably a horrendous crime that must be punished, but a rave party protected by an electric fence next to an open-air prison is not as benign as a concert in a Paris theater. In the 1980s, in divided Berlin, rock concerts were organized right next to the Berlin Wall so that the people on the other side could hear. The message was straightforward: we would like to be with you, and this concert is a protest against the wall that separates us. But the rave party in the Negev took place in total indifference to what was happening beyond the electric fence. Gaza did not exist. Sooner or later the pressure cooker would explode.

The October 7 attack was an atrocity. Carefully planned, it was far more deadly than the Deir Yassin massacre or the other slaughters carried out by the Irgun in 1948. It was intended to spread terror, and, it goes without saying, nothing can justify it; but it must be analyzed, not simply deplored. Debates about the relationship between means and ends are not new.[2] The dialectic uniting them implies that a goal may not be attained by any and all means; on the contrary, every end requires appropriate means: freedom can't be won by consciously killing innocent people. In this case, inappropriate and reprehensible means were used as part of a legitimate struggle against an illegal, inhuman, and unacceptable occupation. As Antonio Guterrez, secretary general of the United Nations, has pointed out, the events of October 7 "did not happen in a vacuum." It was an extreme consequence of decades of occupation, colonization, dispossession, and humiliation. All forms of peaceful protest had been bloodily suppressed, Israel sabotaged the Oslo Accords from the outset, and the Palestinian Authority, entirely powerless, has become a kind of auxiliary police for the IDF in the West Bank.

In October 2023, Israel was "negotiating peace" with its Arab neighbors on the backs of the Palestinians and quietly pursuing its objective, openly acknowledged today, of expanding the settlements in the West Bank. Suddenly, Hamas called the whole process into question by asserting itself as a protagonist in the conflict. Its attack, dealing a violent blow inside Israel's borders, revealed Israel's vulnerability. After the Hamas attack, the Palestinians showed that they were capable of going on the offensive and not just suffering passively.[3] It may seem unfortunate from the perspective of the United States or Europe, but a part of Palestinian public opinion rejoiced in the October 7 massacre. For once, terror, impotence, fear, and humiliation were in the other camp. And schadenfreude is a human emotion, like the wan smile on the faces of Auschwitz inmates when they heard the news of the bombing of German cities.

Palestinian violence has the force of despair. It springs from "a community of pain and resentment," as Jean-Pierre Filiu has written, forged by decades of ruthless occupation that has turned the Gaza Strip into "an open-air prison." This description, he added, "was actually far from the mark since, in any jailhouse, detainees are not supposed to be shot at or bombed except in the case of a full-fledged riot. In Gaza, Israeli raids, whether 'targeted' or not, remained a regular occurrence."[4] The point is not to idealize the violence, but to understand its roots. Hamas is popular among a large number of Palestinians, that's a fact. It is particularly popular among the young people in the West Bank, where Hamas can't

assert its influence through coercion. It's popular because it fights against the occupation. Founded in 1987
in the wake of the First Intifada as the political and military arm of the Muslim Brotherhood, the largest of the
conservative Islamist movements in the Middle East,
Hamas gained strength after the failure of the Oslo Accords. In 2000, the Second Intifada gave it a new influx
of energy. In 2006, Hamas was elected to power in Gaza,
replacing a largely discredited Palestinian Authority. It
has condemned the Holocaust and anti-Semitism, declaring that its fight is not against the Jews but against
the Zionist state.[5] In 2017, its new charter abandoned the
plan of destroying Israel and adopted the idea of a Palestinian state within the 1967 borders, that is, the West
Bank, Gaza, and East Jerusalem.[6] The Israeli response
was the March 2018 massacre mentioned above. While
Hamas was developing a political strategy to replace its
ineffectual military option, Israel shut the door on any
form of dialogue, Netanyahu declared his opposition to
a Palestinian state, and his government expanded the
colonies in the West Bank, moved the capital to Jerusalem, and "froze" Gaza. October 7 was the inevitable
blowback.

All Hamas's leaders, many of whom were born
in refugee camps, have seen the inside of Israeli pris-
ons, some of them for years on end; all have suffered

assassination attempts, and most of them have been killed, notably those living in Gaza, in targeted bombings where they died with their wives and children. Ismail Haniyeh, the chief political leader of Hamas living in exile in Qatar, has lost sixty members of his family, among them children and grandchildren killed by drone attacks. This is the backdrop for Hamas's extremism. Should we criticize the fundamentalist, authoritarian, antidemocratic, homophobic, misogynistic, and reactionary nature of this movement? Unquestionably. In a free society, Hamas would undoubtedly be the Left's main enemy. As things stand now, Hamas is putting up military resistance to a genocide in progress. Palestinians who chafed under its dictatorship now look on it indulgently. You don't shoot the leaders who are defending your besieged city. During World War II, the historian Anne Applebaum tells us, many *zeks*, inmates of the Soviet gulags, asked to enlist in the Red Army. The prisoners, she explains, were "moved by patriotic feelings." As many people testified, "the worst thing was not being able to join the fight at the front."[7] A large number of Western intellectuals declared their admiration for Stalin, and even the more insightful, who denounced his totalitarian tendencies, were in no doubt about the need to support the USSR in combating the German invasion.[8] Once again, the historical contexts may differ, but the sympathy Hamas enjoys among Palestinians and others in the Arab world comes from similar motivations.

The attack on October 7, which killed hundreds of Israeli civilians, obviously qualifies as a terrorist act. There was no need to murder and injure civilians, and such acts have always hurt the Palestinian cause. The attack was a crime that nothing can justify, and it must be condemned. Yet if this means of action necessarily calls for our disapproval, the legitimacy of a resistance to occupation—sanctioned by international law—cannot therefore be called into question. Even if that resistance is armed.

National liberation movements have often advocated and practiced terrorism, and the Hamas militiaman fits the classic definition of a partisan quite well: an irregular fighter with a strong ideological motivation, rooted in a particular territory, and operating in the midst of a population that protects him. Hamas fighters, who move quickly and easily through a maze of underground passages, have a "tellurian" quality that makes them, if not invulnerable, at least hard to eradicate.[9] That's why the Israeli army is killing everyone, relying on AI algorithms, and taking prisoners, many of them teenagers, whom it locks away for months if not years. All that Hamas can do, not being a state, is to take hostages and launch rockets. Hamas's terrorism is just the dialectic twin of Israeli state terrorism. Terrorism is never pretty, but the terrorism of the oppressed is generated by that of their oppressor. Terrorists who kill children on a kibbutz are hateful; snipers who kill children on a street or blow up a humanitarian aid convoy are just as hateful; both must be condemned. But this doesn't mean we can equate the violence of a national liberation movement with that of an occupying army. They do not have equal legitimacy. The crimes of the former stem from the use of illegitimate means; those of the latter from the very purpose they serve.

The concept of terrorism is controversial and hard to define. The only formal difference between the fighters in a terrorist group or organization and soldiers in a regular army is a legal one: the former do not have the legal status conferred by belonging to a state. The difference often manifests itself in dress. Ideologies, values, morals, and methods of action can vary widely among both terrorist groups and armies, but armies generally have far more powerful means of destruction.[10] The supposed ethical superiority of armies over terrorist groups has been refuted countless times in history. These are some fairly obvious considerations that are worth recalling in these times—an era inaugurated on September 11, 2001—when the war against terrorism has become a kind of categorical imperative, immune from critical argument or interpretation.

In a famous chapter of *The Wretched of the Earth* (first published in 1961), Frantz Fanon describes the liberating nature of violence when exercised by the subjugated: "The colonized man finds his freedom in and through violence."[11] In his introduction to the book, Jean-Paul Sartre goes even further, endorsing anti-colonial violence unreservedly. October 7 marked the spectacular backlash of Palestinian violence after the failure of the Oslo Accords. This is not to say that such actions will be effective or inevitable, but it would be hard to deny that it was a consequence of this failure of diplomacy, this shipwreck willed by Netanyahu and consciously perpetuated by every Israeli government for thirty years. It would be thoughtless to rejoice in the violent Hamas reprisal, but the significance of this historic turning point cannot be underestimated. To explain it away as Islamic fanaticism, the barbarity of Hamas, or age-old anti-Semitism would be a shameful evasion, a way of hiding behind prejudices. In the terrible competition between Israeli violence and Palestinian violence, the former unequivocally wins. But Vietnam, and more recently Afghanistan, have taught us that in war the balance of power is not measured solely by military might, and that armed resistance can bring down a far more powerful adversary, when its domination has become so illegitimate that it proves costly, ineffective, and counterproductive. Israeli leaders and their allies do not seem to have learned this lesson.

In *At the Mind's Limits* (1966), Jean Améry writes that in the Nazi camps, "Physical violence is the sole means for restoring a disjointed personality." It was through violence and not by subjectively appealing to his "abstract humanity" that this Auschwitz inmate could best affirm his humanity: "I gave concrete social form to my dignity by punching a human face."[12] One of the hardest tasks, Améry wrote in a 1969 essay on Frantz Fanon, is to transform sterile, vengeful violence into liberating, revolutionary violence:

Freedom and dignity must be attained by way of violence, in order to be freedom and dignity. Again: why? I'm not afraid to introduce here the untouchable and abjected concept of revenge, which Fanon avoids. Vengeful violence, in contradiction to oppressive violence, creates equality in negativity: in suffering. Repressive violence is the denial of equality and thus of man. Revolutionary violence is eminently *humane.* I know it is difficult to get used to the thought, but it is important to consider it at least in the non-binding space of speculation. To extend Fanon's metaphor: the oppressed, the colonized, the concentration camp inmate, perhaps even the Latin

American wage slave, *must be able to see the feet of the oppressor* in order to be able to become a human being, and, conversely, in order for the oppressor, who is not human in this role, to become human as well.[13]

One needs to move beyond this terrible, purely negative stage of "equality of suffering," but as Frantz Fanon writes, violence on the part of the oppressed is "a cleansing force."[14] Decades of memory politics focused almost exclusively on the suffering of the victims, aiming to present the cause of the oppressed as the triumph of innocence, have obscured a reality that has seemed obvious at other times. The oppressed rebel by resorting to violence, and this violence is neither pretty nor idyllic, and is sometimes even horrifying. In a remarkable book on the history of slavery, the American anthropologist Saidiya Hartman quotes the testimony of a French colonist in the West Indies:

The unhappy day was the 23rd of November, 1733, at three in the morning. Mr. Soetman's Negroes, assisted by others, broke down their master's door, while he was sleeping, ordered him to get up, and, after having him stripped naked, forced him to sing and dance. Then, after having run a sword through his body, they cut his head off, cut open his body, and washed themselves in his blood. To this execution, they added that of his daughter Hissing, thirteen years old, by slaughtering her on top of her stepfather's body.[15]

This horrific scene, Hartman reports, was "the inaugural act of their rebellion."

In 1966, the Venice Film Festival awarded the Golden Lion to Gillo Pontecorvo's *The Battle of Algiers*, a masterpiece that has assumed a place beyond the history of film in the canon of postcolonial culture. A crucial scene in the film shows Algerian women, having put on makeup and dressed in Western clothes, going into cafés frequented by French youths to plant bombs. Killing civilians, as deplorable as it may be, has always been the weapon of the weak in asymmetric wars. The Algerian FLN used it, but so did Nelson Mandela's ANC, the PLO before Oslo, Vietnam's FNL, who targeted the Saigon brothels patronized by American servicemen, and even the aforementioned Irgun, who, in the days before Israel's statehood, set bombs targeting the British (the attack on the King David Hotel in Jerusalem, in July 1946, killed ninety-one people and wounded forty-five, including British nationals but also Arabs and Jews). The practice of targeting civilians was used in Europe as well, though we tend to forget it, from the Spanish Civil War to the French Resistance in World War II.

In Italy, since the "Years of Lead" of the 1960s to the 1980s, and in the rest of the world since September 11, 2001, something has changed in the collective unconscious and even in our vocabulary, especially after the Islamist attacks in Paris in 2015. Decades of peace, democracy, and relative prosperity have led us to internalize the rejection of violence—the advent of peaceful customs, which Norbert Elias identified as an essential feature of the civilizing process—by extending our norms to contexts very different from our own.[16] The propensity is understandable, but it is anachronistic and wrong. In his book on the Italian Resistance as a civil war, Claudio Pavone notes that the words "terror" and "terrorism" were quite common in Resistance texts, used uninhibitedly and with none of the echoes that resonate today after the Years of Lead in Italy (and, one could add today, after Islamic terrorism in many countries).[17] In his masterly history of the Gruppi di azione patriottica (Patriotic Action Groups, known as GAP), the partisans who led the armed rebellion in the cities, Santo Peli has made a painstaking study of how the attacks against the occupier were organized, attacks not just against the headquarters but within civil society itself. In many cities, the GAP organized spectacular terrorist strikes, detonating bombs in bars, restaurants, movie theaters, and brothels frequented by the enemy. By late 1944, this activity had reached such proportions that the Communist Party, in a letter written by Pietro Secchia, asked them to "desist from this form of combat, which is losing us the people's sympathy."[18] Giorgio Bocca, who before becoming a famous journalist was a partisan in the Piedmont, described the Resistance's terrorism as "an act of revolutionary morale," highlighting a number of aspects that would generally be condemned today. The terrorism of the Resistance, he wrote, "was not intended to prevent the occupier's terrorism but to provoke and exacerbate it. It was premeditated self-mutilation: it sought wounds, punishment, reprisals; it aimed at winning over the undecided, at deepening the gulf of hatred. It was a ruthless pedagogy, a cruel lesson. The communists rightly considered it necessary and were the only ones capable of delivering it right then."[19]

In fighting against the German occupation, the partisans of the Main d'oeuvre immigrée (MOI)—the section of the French Communist Party reserved for immigrants, mostly Jews from Central Europe, Armenians, Spanish republicans, and Italian anti-fascists—also used terrorist methods. Denounced at the time by the Germans as "Judeo-Bolshevist terrorists," MOI fighters, whose leader, Missak Manouchian, lies today in the Pantheon in Paris, carried out attacks in French towns and cities. They not only killed officers and laid ambushes, they also set off bombs in the restaurants and cafés where Germans gathered.[20] In *L'Armée du crime*, the fine film made by Robert Guédiguian about the Manouchian group and the Affiche Rouge (Red Poster), there is an episode that dramatizes the doubts and hesitations that Resistance fighters felt when executing a plan that called for civilian deaths. We watch Celestino Alfonso enter a hotel where a Kommandantur reception is underway. There is an orchestra, people dancing, soldiers, officers, and prostitutes. Alfonso makes the rounds, then decides against planting his bomb and exits the hotel. He doesn't want to kill innocent lives; he just can't do it. Marcel Rayman decides to replace him on the spot, but he can't do it either. The leader, Manouchian, is upset; the group leaves without accomplishing their mission. It's not unreasonable to think that these dilemmas were even more difficult in reality than they seem in the film. In fact, Santo Peli quotes a nineteen-year-old *gappista* from Rome, Maria Teresa Regard, who describes her sense of trauma and "deep discouragement" after making her first attack on December 16, 1943:

> The three of us, Francesco, Pasquale, and I, followed a uniformed fascist along a stretch of the via Cola di Rienzo. It was Pasquale who shot him. Seeing the fascist collapse on the sidewalk, and realizing he was a young man more or less our

age, Pasquale stood there paralyzed, convulsed
with tremors and vomiting. Francesco and I had
to support him under the arms and forcibly lead
him away.[21]

The line between terrorist and combatant is not always clear-cut; often the two figures overlap. The glossy
image of the combatant as a shining hero is a myth.
The stereotypical image of the terrorist as a cruel and
fanatical beast, crazed by the heady fumes of blood and
death, is also false in the majority of cases.

Since time immemorial, rape has been a particularly despicable weapon of war, used by virtually all
armies, including those engaged in just wars. In recent decades, it has been used in the former Yugoslavia, Afghanistan, Iraq, Nigeria, and Ukraine, to
mention only a few well-known cases. In May 1945,
the entrance of the Red Army into Berlin was expe-
rienced as a nightmare by tens of thousands of German women. Red Army leaflets urged soldiers to treat
them as spoils of war.[22] Today, according to several
witnesses, rapes have been committed both by Hamas
combatants and by Israeli soldiers—no proof has been
forthcoming, because, having spread the most fantasti-
cal rumors about Hamas's atrocities, the IDF has pre-
vented any investigation into the subject. According to
Pramila Patten, head of the U.N. office responsible for

investigating sexual violence in armed conflicts, numerous reports agree that these rapes occurred. We do
not know whether the rapes were planned by Hamas,
or encouraged by the IDF, notably during the interro-
gations carried out after October 7. What is certain is
that the sexual violence committed by the Palestinian
combatants has received much more media coverage
than that of Israeli soldiers, as numerous Arab femi-
nists have noted.[23] Is there any difference in this realm
between soldiers and "terrorists"? The media hype over
the Hamas rapes coincided, as it happens, with a revealing case of censorship. The novel by the Palestinian
author Adania Shibli, *Minor Detail* (2020), whose prize
at the Frankfurt Book Fair in October 2023 was canceled by censors with very exacting moral standards,
is about the rape and murder of a young Palestinian
woman by Israeli soldiers during the Nakba in 1949.[24]

There is something curious about the plethora of
articles and newscasts where "Hamas" is inevitably
paired with the qualifier "barbaric." Terrorist attacks
horrify us, provoking outrage and disapproval, but
our era, so quick to lapse into the rhetoric of human
rights, is surprisingly jaded when it comes to the violence of carpet bombings, targets highlighted on com-
puter screens, smart bombs, and "surgical" strikes
that annihilate cities with millions of inhabitants. Our
"human rights" are regularly invoked to legitimize our

"humanitarian wars," and war demands the sacred union, but when Francesca Albanese, U.N. special correspondent for the Palestinian territories, described genocide on the part of Israel, she was accused of complicity with terrorism.

The October 7 massacre must therefore be condemned, and the fundamentalist ideology of Hamas must be criticized, but to deny that this group belongs to the Palestinian resistance—as some have done, pointing to its terrorist element—is irresponsible. We can issue judgments, formulate expressions of support, criticism, or condemnation, but we have no standing to rule on whether a given person or group belongs to the Palestinian resistance. Should the communist combatants—including the heroic MOI—be denied status as members of the French Resistance on the grounds that their party supported a totalitarian ideology and regime? We could discuss Hamas's origins and its evolution, or the circumstances that enabled its development, notably when Israel released its leaders from jail and encouraged its growth in order to weaken the PLO and divide the Palestinian camp.[25] But the basic fact is that this is a movement whose combatants are battling against an army of occupation.

Western nations deny Hamas the status of a legitimate actor (they negotiate with it through Egypt and Qatar), but they show exquisite courtesy when it comes to meeting Netanyahu and his government, although they have now been designated as criminals (for war crimes and crimes against humanity), on a par with Hamas's leaders, by a prosecutor at the International Criminal Court in The Hague. None of these countries has ever called for the release of Marwan Barghouti, who has been detained for the past twenty years and is the only Palestinian leader with the legitimacy to conduct genuine negotiations with Israel on behalf of Gaza and the West Bank. The Western countries call for the observance of humanitarian law, but they refuse to condemn an offensive aimed at perpetuating and extending an illegal occupation. The double standard that they have adopted with respect to Ukraine and Palestine—first invoking international law against Russia, then ignoring it when Israel tramples it underfoot—provokes the outrage and incomprehension of the entire planet.

7

Crossed Memories

Decades of occupation could only engender frustration and violence, not a desire for dialogue and mutual recognition. Negotiation would have to be imposed on the parties from outside, but clearly the nations that could do so have chosen not to. More than twenty years ago, during the Second Intifada, Edward Said pointed to the impossibility of a dialogue between two such radically opposed visions of reality. In 1948, the Palestinians were dispossessed and uprooted, he wrote, while Israel was announcing its newly won independence; the Palestinians were stripped of their land and expelled by the hundreds of thousands, while Israel took back land it claimed belonged to the Jews by biblical decree; the Palestinians endured decades of occupation and denial of their rights, while Israel claimed to be acting on behalf of a people of victims. A unilateral narrative celebrates the history of the one and denies or ignores the history of the other. For a

long time, in parallel with the formal recognition of
Israel as a nation, first by the U.N. in 1948, and con-
firmed in the next decade by reparation treaties with
West Germany, the national character of the Palestinians was denied, as they were relegated to the generic
Arab world.[1] While Palestine remained something abstract and elusive, Israel gradually acquired a symbolic
dimension that was reinforced by the emergence of a
historical consciousness of the Holocaust on a global
scale.

In Europe and the United States, Israel is never
treated as an actual country, but rather as "an idea or
talisman of some sort,"[2] the telltale sign of a guilty conscience, whose expiation can be subcontracted out, as
always happens in an unequal and hierarchical world.
Israel benefited from this change of mood in international opinion and never fixed its own borders, which
became provisional and expansive. It was the Palestinians who paid, and who continue to pay, Europe's debt
toward the Jews.

Now integrated into the Western world, Israel has
borrowed the West's language and its old racial prejudices to apply them to the Palestinians. Frantz Fanon
has described the Manicheanism of the colonial world,
where the colonized are forever dehumanized and
made into animals: "The terms the settler uses when he
mentions the natives are zoological terms."[3] This same

language has taken root in Israel today. Defense Minister Yoav Gallant, for instance, declared that Israel was fighting "human animals" in Gaza.[4] In 1983, Rafael Eitan, the army's chief of staff, was already describing the Palestinians as "roaches in a bottle."[5] Anyone familiar with the history of anti-Semitism from Wilhelm Marr and Édouard Drumont onward can easily trace the genealogy of this rhetoric. By a ricochet effect, the rich arsenal of anti-Semitic stereotypes created in Europe at the end of the nineteenth century has migrated to the Middle East, where it is thriving—including its most grotesque forms, such as *The Protocols of the Elders of Zion*, readily available on the Internet and in the bookstores of major Arab cities.

This offshoot of European anti-Semitism now flourishing in the Middle East supports the Zionist narrative that it's not the decades of oppression and the denial of Palestinians' rights that are behind the October 7 attack, but the age-old anti-Semitism of the Palestinians themselves, their ancestral and unquenchable hatred of the Jews. The attack has now been styled a "pogrom," as though Hamas were in power and the Israelis an oppressed minority, like the Jews in tsarist times. This is a rewriting of history, something Benjamin Netanyahu has tried his hand at several times, notably by claiming that Hitler took his inspiration from the grand mufti of Jerusalem and that Hamas—like

Arafat in the past—was just a reincarnation of Hitler.[6] Nothing new here.

Exasperated by the sheer number of mythological tales and the violence they fuel, some intellectuals have tried to trace them back to their source. In the late 1980s, the Israeli journalist Yehuda Elkana, who witnessed scenes of atrocity during the 1982 Lebanon War, suggested that the propensity stemmed from a "profound existential fear [...] tending to make the Jewish people the eternal victims of a hostile world." This belief, clearly still present forty years later, was, in his eyes, "Hitler's paradoxical and tragic victory." Noting that Nazism still weighed on people's minds, he proposed exploring the virtues of forgetting: "The rule of historical remembrance," he wrote, "must be uprooted from our lives."[7]

When memory becomes so distorted, one is tempted to discover the virtues of forgetfulness. Anticipating Yehuda Elkana, Primo Levi gave an interview to the Italian daily *La Repubblica* a day after the Sabra and Shatila massacre in which he recognized the "deep existential fear" of Jews, but refused to use it as an excuse: "I know that Israel was founded by people like me, only less fortunate. Men with Auschwitz numbers tattooed on their arms, men who were homeless and stateless, who escaped the horrors of World War II and found a house and a homeland there. I know all that.

But I also know that it's Begin's favorite argument. And I deny the validity of that argument."[8] As far as Primo Levi was concerned, the Holocaust did not give Israel ontological innocence. He viewed Begin as an outright "fascist," a label he thought Begin would in fact happily accept.[9] But today, compared to Netanyahu, Begin would look like a moderate.

I'm no longer certain after forty years, or two generations, that Elkana's diagnosis of Israeli mental life is still accurate. Menachem Begin lived the Israeli invasion of Lebanon in a state of mythological exaltation, seeing himself as leading a Jewish army to free the Warsaw ghetto in 1943. The Zionist supremacists of today are different; they are not even the children of the founders of the Israeli state, in whom Primo Levi saw companions in misfortune. Today's Jewish supremacists are like our fascists in the West who beat up a Black or an Arab man to prove their virility. Twenty years ago, the British American historian Tony Judt noted with despair that after the Six-Day War in 1967, and even more after the First Intifada, Israel had undergone a dark transformation:

> Today [Israel] presents a ghastly image: a place where sneering eighteen-year-olds with M16 carbines taunt helpless old men ("security measures"); where bulldozers regularly flatten whole

apartment blocks ("collective punishment"); where helicopters fire rockets into residential streets ("targeted assassination"); where subsidized settlers frolic in grass-fringed swimming pools, oblivious to Arab children a few meters away who fester and rot in the worst slums on the planet; and where retired generals and cabinet ministers speak openly of [...] cleansing the land of its Arab cancer.[10]

Elkana's reaction is understandable, even if it's now dated; but forgetting can't be decreed—memory can only be censored. You can't erase a past whose ghosts inhabit the present without needing to be summoned. Beyond their debatable and approximate nature, given the difference between times, contexts, and actors, a few historical analogies spontaneously come to mind: the destruction of Gaza by the IDF recalls the razing of the Warsaw ghetto by General Stroop in 1943, and the combatants leaping out of tunnels to strike at an occupying army that sees them as "animals" inevitably suggests the Jewish fighters in the ghetto. True, the IDF's flags bear a Star of David, not a swastika, but that doesn't make its soldiers innocent. The deeply troubling images that these soldiers post on social media, proudly and hilariously displaying themselves next to humiliated Palestinians, recall the unconscionable souvenir photos that German soldiers of the Wehrmacht took in Poland and Belarus, where we see them smiling beside the hanged bodies of partisans.[11] Given the many videos posted to social networks (despite the censorship of the major channels) showing the bodies of children, humanitarian aid workers, and civilians killed by snipers or drones, then carted off with bulldozers, and given the discovery of mass graves filled with hundreds of corpses, their hands tied, the impression of a Holocaust by bullets and a planned massacre grows ever stronger. Someone might object that it's not the same thing, but it looks as though Israel is doing everything it can to erase the difference. Netanyahu is not Hitler, and his government is not a Nazi regime, this is obvious. Nonetheless, after decades of obsessively comparing the PLO—and now Hamas—to the Nazis, this juxtaposition now risks backfiring with a boomerang effect.

8

From the River to the Sea

October 7 and the war in Gaza mark the definitive failure of the Oslo Accords. Far from laying the groundwork for a lasting peace and the coexistence of two independent states, the accords were sabotaged from the start by Israel, which has used them as the basis for settling the West Bank, annexing East Jerusalem, and isolating the Palestinian Authority, now reduced to a corrupt and discredited shadow entity. And this failure signals the end of the two-state solution. Still vaguely subscribed to by Europeans and the Biden administration—who never thought to consult with the Palestinians on the subject—the plan would only have resulted in a Bantustan or two for Palestine, guarded by the Israeli military. After the annexation of East Jerusalem, into which 220,000 settlers have moved, the installation of 500,000 settlers in the West Bank, and the destruction of Gaza, the two-state scenario has become objectively impossible. Moreover, the

Israeli government doesn't want two states. It wants to annex the West Bank and carry out the ethnic cleansing of Gaza. As we saw earlier, several members of the government have explicitly said as much.

So what can we hope for? Twenty years ago, Edward Said declared that a secular two-nation state—a democratic republic capable of guaranteeing total equality of rights to both its Jewish and its Palestinian citizens—was the only possible road to peace. That's in fact the meaning of the slogan *From the river to the sea, Palestine will be free* and its variants *From the river to the sea, we demand equality* and *From the river to the sea, everyone must be free*—which most of the media insists on characterizing as anti-Semitic,[1] repeating an accusation that goes back to the days of the Yom Kippur War, when the B'nai B'rith Anti-Defamation League started to denounce a new anti-Semitism on the left of the political spectrum.[2]

The accusation, all the same, seems fairly odd. Why couldn't the Palestinians be free between the Jordan River and the Mediterranean? Perhaps because this is Israel's "vital space," according to a formula favored by extremists in Netanyahu's government?[3] Another role reversal. At the start of the twentieth century, when the German geographer Friedrich Ratzel invented the concept of "vital space" (*Lebensraum*), pan-Germanists considered the borders established by international law to be pure abstractions, the product of disembodied Jewish thought, and set up in opposition to it an idea of space that was not only geographical but existential and biological, a space made to be shaped by a people's vital force.[4] This was the ideological origin of their expansionist policies, well before Nazism appropriated the concept. Today, the idea of "vital space" has been adopted by Zionism, which since the birth of Israel has constantly extended the country's borders, in defiance of international law. This is the territorial aspect of the Zionist theological-political plan, which holds that Jewish ownership of this space was ordained in the Scriptures.

Many U.S. politicians for whom the idea of the United States as an exclusively white and Christian country would be racist and insane, or who consider the Islamic Republic of Iran a historical anachronism, are nonetheless staunch defenders of Israel, a state built on ethnic and religious foundations. In fact, since a Knesset vote in 2018, Israel has become the "Nation-State of the Jewish people." In Italy, the most faithful allies of the "Jewish state" of Israel are to be found in the ranks of the xenophobic right, those who refuse on principle to introduce *jus soli*, the right of citizenship to those born in Italy of immigrant parents.

Under its Law of Return, Israel welcomes all diasporic Jews, but it denies Palestinians expelled in 1948 and their descendants the right to return. Israel is a democratic state for its citizens but a military dictatorship for Palestinians in the occupied territories, who have been deprived of their rights. In reality, as Amnon Raz-Krakotzkin has noted, Israel is not a "nation-state" but an "ongoing process of redemption" based on a unique combination of theology and colonialism. It's a state that embodies "a perpetual goal of immigration, population, and Judaism," from which Arabs are by definition excluded.[5] Israel, Raz-Krakotzkin observes, is ultimately neither a nation-state in the traditional sense of the term nor a democratic state. Israel's goal, Edward Said wrote prophetically, was to make Palestinians invisible. That goal is tacitly shared by the United States, the European Union, and even the Arab countries, who were recently on the verge of recognizing Israel (in the wake of the Abraham Accords, which the United Arab Emirates, Bahrain, Morocco, and Sudan have already signed with Israel), without regard for the Palestinians. October 7 reminded them that the Palestinians haven't disappeared.

Quite clearly, the future of Israel and Palestine must be decided by the men and women living there. Yet peace-minded outsiders might nonetheless point to a few lessons their own history has taught them. A two-state solution could be put in place today only at the cost of a reciprocal program of ethnic cleansing:

expelling Jewish colonizers from the West Bank, establishing borders within Jerusalem by creating exclusive ethnic neighborhoods, and finally finding a solution for the two million Palestinians who currently hold Israeli citizenship. Is this a rational solution for a land shared by equal numbers of Jews and Palestinians? Even imagining the creation of a genuinely sovereign Palestinian state, this split into two national entities, each with an ethnically and religiously homogeneous population, would be a step backward in history. The situation could even take an extreme and cartoonish turn if it came to two fundamentalist states facing off against each other, one Zionist, the other Islamic. No fruitful exchange between the cultures, languages, and religions sharing this land could occur. As the history of Central Europe and the Balkans in the twentieth century has shown, the results would be tragic. That's why many of the actors in this conflict see no other possible course than a binational state in which Israelis and Palestinians, Jews, Muslims, and Christians would coexist on an equal footing. Today, this option seems unattainable, but if we think in the long term, it seems logical and coherent.

The idea of a binational state is in no way anti-Semitic, and it certainly doesn't equate with wanting to expel Jews from Palestine. Israel is not only a state, it is also a structured nation with a living and dynamic

culture that has every right to exist, but the future of
this nation is threatened by the political entity govern-
ing and representing it today. In the global world of the
twenty-first century, a state based on an exclusive eth-
nicity and religion is an aberration, in Israel-Palestine
as elsewhere.

Why would a binational Israeli-Palestinian state be
impossible or irrational? In the throes of World War II,
the idea of building a European federation combining
Germany, France, Italy, Belgium, and the Netherlands
would have seemed strange and naïve. But ten years
later, the process of building Europe had started—
about which much could certainly be said and pos-
sibly even objected to—but by the end of the process
the idea of a war between Germany, Italy, and France
had become quite simply absurd. Why would the same
not be true in the Middle East? History is littered with
prejudices, uprooted and discarded, that in retrospect
appear to be thoughtless anachronisms. Sometimes
tragedies serve to open up new horizons. The idea of a
federal or binational state was for a long time the plan
supported by the PLO and a branch of the Israeli left,
Matzpen.

Before the founding of Israel, that concept was at
the heart of what was called "cultural Zionism," whose
leading figures included Robert Weltsch, Gershom
Scholem, Hannah Arendt, Martin Buber, and Judah

Magnes, one of the founders of the Hebrew University
of Jerusalem. All these intellectuals rejected Herzl's
political Zionism at the time of Israel's founding, and
several of them considered the formation of a Hebrew state to be a historic error. The correspondence
between Arendt and Scholem documents this rift. In
1946, Scholem couldn't stand the "tone" of Arendt's
anti-Zionist position statements—she wrote that "a
Jewish national state would be a dangerous and stu-
pid joke."[6] Before the founding of Israel, Zionism was a
composite movement, host to a sometimes paradoxical
diversity of beliefs. It included spiritualists with liber-
tarian leanings such as Scholem, declared anarchists
such as Abba Gordin, Marxists such as Ber Borochov,
and, by contrast, nationalists nursing a sympathy for
fascism such as Vladimir Jabotinsky. All these different
strands were occluded or largely subsumed by Herzl's
political Zionism, of which Ben-Gurion considered
himself the heir, and from which the leaders of today's
Likud Party claim direct descent.[7] What occasioned
this change and locked it in place was the 1948 Arab-
Israeli War. Today, most of the strands of belief mentioned above would be branded anti-Zionist.

In 1950, shortly after the first Arab-Israeli war,
Arendt wrote that the great tragedy to arise from this
conflict was "the creation of a new category of homeless

people, the Arab refugees."[8] Israel's victory, far from ensuring its security, had laid the foundations for a permanent crisis. Once the war was won, she wrote,

its end would find the unique possibilities and the unique achievements of Zionism in Palestine destroyed. The land that would come into being would be something quite other than the dream of world Jewry, Zionist and non-Zionist. The "victorious" Jews would live surrounded by an entirely hostile population, secluded inside ever-threatened borders, absorbed with physical self-defense to a degree that would submerge all other interests and activities. The growth of a Jewish culture would cease to be the concern of the whole people; social experiments would have to be discarded as impractical luxuries; political thought would center around military strategy; economic development would be determined exclusively by the needs of war. And all this would be the fate of a nation that—no matter how many immigrants it could still absorb and how far it extended its boundaries (the whole of Palestine and Transjordan is the insane Revisionist demand)— would still remain a very small people greatly outnumbered by hostile neighbors.[9]

This landscape, which Arendt conjured up as a night-mare, is today before our eyes. It was precisely to avoid this impasse that intellectuals who supported the creation of a "Jewish national homeland" in Palestine rejected the Zionist vision of a Jewish state, proposing a binational state instead. This, Judah Magnes believed, was the only good option, which he described in probably naïve but also refreshing and visionary terms:

> What a boon to mankind it would be if the Jews and Arabs of Palestine were to strive together in friendship and partnership to make this Holy Land into a thriving peaceful Switzerland in the heart of this ancient highway between East and West. This would have incalculable political and spiritual influence in all the Middle East and far beyond. A binational Palestine could become a beacon of peace in the world.[10]

Magnes imagined a Palestine that was free, from the Jordan River to the sea. Should he be labeled retrospectively an anti-Semite?

Twenty years ago, Edward Said raised the following question: "Where are the Israeli equivalents of Nadine Gordimer, Andre Brink, Athol Fugard, those white writers who spoke out unequivocally and with unambiguous clarity against the evils of South African apartheid?"[11] The silence is just as deafening today, broken only by a few isolated voices. We have seen impressive demonstrations calling for Netanyahu's removal, but they did not denounce the massacre in Gaza; they only demanded more effective actions for the release of the hostages and the removal of Netanyahu for corruption. Similar demonstrations took place last year, but they showed complete indifference to the powder keg building in Gaza and a growing habituation to colonization of the occupied territories, now accepted as normal and irreversible. We have not heard a voice comparable to that of the philosopher Yeshahayu Leibowitz, who in 1982 called the Lebanon War a "Judeo-Nazi policy."[12] The violent trauma of October 7 seems to have paralyzed people's consciences, even if some courageous voices have been raised, sometimes in spectacular fashion. During the 2024 Berlin Film Festival, Yuval Abraham, codirector with the Palestinian Basel Adra of the documentary *No Other Land*, spoke the following words as he received his prize for best documentary: "I am Israeli, Basel is Palestinian. In two days we will go back to a land where we are not equal. […] This situation of apartheid between us, this inequality, it has to end."[13] The voices against the war are much more numerous and audible among the Jews of the Diaspora, who are obviously not responsible for the massacre, yet many of them have felt impelled to

say that they do not consider themselves represented
by Israel, which pretends to act in their name. In the
United States, this is probably the dominant outlook
among the younger generation. In New York, the organization Jewish Voice for Peace has occupied Grand
Central, the city's main railway station, the Manhat-
tan Bridge, and Liberty Island; its black T-shirts with
the slogan *Not in our name* have been extraordinarily
successful. In Italy, an open letter signed by many of
the country's most important Jewish figures posed this
fundamental question: "What use is memory today if
it does not contribute to stopping the manufacture of
death in Gaza and the West Bank? Not to ask this question is to turn the Day of Remembrance into an empty,
ritualistic celebration."[14] In France, a similar letter
went out, over the names of intellectuals whose parents or grandparents had been persecuted or deported.
Remarkable for its insight, generosity, and, in the current climate, courage, the text starts with these words:

> After fifty-seven years of occupation, marked
> by humiliation, expulsion from their homes,
> arbitrary imprisonment, multiple killings, the
> settlement of colonies, and the repeated failure
> of different peaceful actions, it is perfectly un-
> derstandable that many Palestinian men and
> women refuse to condemn the actions of Hamas

on October 7, regarding it as a legitimate act of resistance against Israel's colonization and state terrorism.

The letter goes on to condemn the Hamas attack and the Israeli massacre that followed, adding that

it is illegitimate and despicable to justify the massacre of tens of thousands of Gazan and West Bank civilians in the name of the genocide of Europe's Jews, in which the Palestinian people had no part. Along with many Jewish men and women around the world, including in Israel, we deny to the Netanyahu government and its supporters the right, using the Holocaust as a pretext, to act in Gaza and the West Bank in our name and that of our ancestors.[15]

Meanwhile, the situation has changed profoundly. Israel has proven to be vulnerable, and because of its destructive fury, devoid of any shred of moral legitimacy. The Palestinian cause has become the flag of the Global South and of a major part of public opinion, especially among young people, including many Jews, in Europe and the United States. What is at stake today is not the existence of Israel but the survival of the Palestinian people. If the war in Gaza were to end in a second Nakba, Israel's legitimacy would be definitively compromised. In that case, neither American weapons, nor the Western media, nor a German reason of state, nor a distorted and profaned memory of the Holocaust, will be able to save it.

Notes

1. Perpetrators and Victims

1 W. G. Sebald, *On the Natural History of Destruction*, tr. Anthea Bell (New York: Modern Library, 2003).

2 Herbert Marcuse, "Heidegger and Marcuse, a Dialogue in Letters" (1948), in *Technology, War and Fascism*, ed. Douglas Kellner (New York: Routledge, 1998), p. 267. Heidegger was not isolated. A similar position was held by Carl Schmitt in his letters and his journal, notably on August 21, 1949. See Carl Schmitt, *Glossarium: Aufzeichungen der Jahre 1947–1951* (Berlin: Duncker & Humblot, 1991), p. 263.

3 At the center of this debate was a work by Jörg Friedrich, *The Fire: The Bombing of Germany, 1940–1945*, tr. Allison Brown (New York: Columbia University Press, 2006).

4 Jean-Pierre Chrétien, "Un nazisme tropical au Rwanda? Image ou logique d'un génocide," *Vingtième siècle*, 1995, 48, pp. 131–142.

5 In the existing huge literature on the Nuremberg trials, the best account remains that of the U.S. prosecutor Telford Taylor, *The Anatomy of the Nuremberg Trials: A Personal Memoir* (New York: Knopf, 1992). On the Katyn massacre, see Anna M. Cienciala, Natalia S. Lebedeva, and Wojciech Materski, eds., *Katyn: A Crime Without Punishment* (New Haven: Yale University Press, 2008).

6 Ernst Nolte, "The Past That Will Not Pass: A Speech That Could Be Written but Not Delivered" (1986), in *Forever in the Shadow of Hitler? Original Documents of the* Historikerstreit, *the Controversy Concerning the Singularity of the Holocaust*, tr. James Knowlton, Truett Cates (Atlantic Highlands, NJ: Humanities Press, 1993), p. 22. On this debate, see Richard Evans, *In Hitler's Shadow: West German Historians and the Attempt to Escape from the Nazi Past* (New York: Pantheon Books, 1989), and Ian Kershaw, *The Nazi Dictatorship: Problems and Perspectives of Interpretation* (New York: Routledge, 1993).

7 On the transformation of conservative thought in Germany, see Enzo Traverso, "Longing for the *Sonderweg*," *New German Critique*, vol. 50, n. 150, 2023, pp. 205–215.

8 Edward W. Said, *From Oslo to Iraq and the Road Map* (New York: Pantheon Books, 2004), p. 197.

9 See the United Nations' official data, published on October 12, 2023, http://www.ochaopt.org/data/casualties.

10 On the origins of the concept of genocide, see Raphael Lemkin, *Lemkin on Genocide*, introduced and edited by Steven L. Jacobs (Langham, MD: Lexington Books, 2012) (1944). On the context that gave rise to the concept of genocide, see Donald Bloxham, *Genocide on Trial: War Crimes Trials and the Formation of Holocaust History and Memory* (New York: Oxford University Press, 2001).

11 Notably Raz Segal and Luigi Daniele, Melanie S. Tanielian, Didier Fassin, Shmuel Lederman, Uğur Ümit Üngör, Elyse Semerdjian, Mark Levene, Zoé Samudzi, Abdelwahab El-Affendi, and Martin Shaw.

12 Raz Segal, "A Textbook Case of Genocide," *Jewish Currents*, Oct. 13, 2023.

13 A. Dirk Moses, "More than Genocide," *Boston Review*, Nov. 14, 2023. Dirk Moses is the author of *The Problems of Genocide: Permanent Security and the Language of Transgression* (New York: Cambridge University Press, 2021).

14 On this statement of Netanyahu's, which was widely reported in the media, see Noah Lanard, "The Dangerous History Behind Netanyahu's Amalek Rhetoric," *Mother Jones*, Nov. 3, 2023.

15 Omer Bartov, *Weaponizing Language: Misuses of Holocaust Memory and the Never Again Syndrome*, Council for Global Cooperation, March 12, 2024, https://cgcinternational .co.in/weaponizing-language-misuses-of-holocaust -memory-and-the-never-again-syndrome.

16 See Janam Mukherjee, *Hungry Bengal: War, Famine, Riots and the End of Empire* (London: HarperCollins, 2015).

17 Bethan McKernan, "Israeli Ministers Attend Conference Calling for 'Voluntary Migration' of Palestinians," *The Guardian*, Jan. 29, 2024.

2. Orientalism

1 For a paradigmatic expression of this cliché—the conflict between civilization (Israel) and barbarism (Hamas)—see Yehuda Bauer, "Hamas and Israel Live in Different Worlds," *The Times of Israel*, Nov. 5, 2023.

2 Edward W. Said, *Orientalism* (New York: Pantheon Books, 1978).

3 Yuval Abraham, "'A Mass Assassination Factory': Inside Israel's Calculated Bombing of Gaza," *+972*, Nov. 30, 2023, https://www.972mag.com/mass-assassination-factory -israel-calculated-bombing-gaza.

4 Yuval Abraham, "Lavender, the AI Machine Directing Israel's Bombing Spree in Gaza," *+972*, April 3, 2024, https:// www.972mag.com/lavender-ai-israeli-army-gaza. See also Benjamin Barthe, "Dans la bande de Gaza, les crimes de guerre sont démultipliés par les algorithmes," *Le Monde*, April 9, 2024.

5 Max Horkheimer and Theodor W. Adorno, *Dialectic of Enlightenment*, ed. Gunzelin Schmid Noerr, tr. Edmund Jephcott (Stanford: Stanford University Press, 2002 [1947]).

6 See Fritz Stern, *Gold and Iron: Bismarck, Bleichröder, and the Building of the German Empire* (New York: Knopf, 1977), and Shulamit Volkov, *Walther Rathenau: Weimar's Fallen Statesman* (New Haven: Yale University Press, 2012).

7 W. E. B. Du Bois, "The Negro and the Warsaw Ghetto" (1952), *The Oxford W. E. B. Du Bois Reader*, ed. Eric Sundquist (New York: Oxford University Press, 1996), p. 625. See Michael Rothberg, *Multidirectional Memory: Remembering the Holocaust in the Age of Decolonization* (Stanford: Stanford University Press, 2009), pp. 111–134.

8 See Sylvain Cypel, *The State of Israel vs. the Jews*, tr. William Rodarmor (New York: Other Press, 2021), notably pp. 91–107, which analyzes this convergence and the birth of an idea of "racial purity" at the heart of Israeli society.

9 Nicole Lapierre, *Causes communes. Des Juifs et des Noirs* (Paris: Stock, 2011), pp. 274–282.

10 Avi Shlaim, *Three Worlds: Memoirs of an Arab-Jew* (London: One World Publications, 2023), pp. 16–17.

11 Yitzhak Laor, *Le nouveau philosémitisme européen et le "camp de la paix" en Israël*, tr. Catherine Neuve-Église and Eric Hazan (Paris: La fabrique, 2007), p. 113. See also Ella Shohat, "Sephardim in Israel: Zionism from the Standpoint of its Jewish Victims" (1988), *On the Arab-Jew, Palestine, and Other Displacements: Selected Writings* (London: Pluto Press, 2017).

12 Ilan Halevi, *A History of the Jews: Ancient and Modern* (London: Zed Books, 1987). See Frantz Fanon, *Black Skin, White Masks*, tr. Richard Philcox (New York: Grove Press, 2008) (1952).

13 See Gilbert Achcar, *Clash of Barbarisms: The Making of the New World Disorder* (London: Saqi Books, 2006).

14 Dan Diner, *Beyond the Conceivable: Studies on Germany, Nazism, and the Holocaust* (Berkeley: University of

California Press, 2000), ch. 12, "Cumulative Contingency: Historicizing Legitimacy in Israeli Discourse," pp. 201–217.

15 Hannah Arendt, "Peace or Armistice in the Near East?" (1950), *The Jewish Writings*, ed. Jerome Kohn and Ron H. Feldman (New York: Schocken Books, 2007), p. 433.

16 Zeev Sternhell, *Founding Myths of Israel: Nationalism, Socialism, and the Making of the Jewish State*, tr. David Maisel (Princeton: Princeton University Press, 1998), pp. 54–55.

17 Zeev Sternhell, *The Anti-Enlightenment Tradition*, tr. David Maisel (New Haven: Yale University Press, 2010).

18 See Elias Sanbar, *"La dernière guerre?" Palestine, 7 octobre 2023–2 avril 2024* (Paris: Gallimard-Tracts, 2024).

19 Aaron-David Gordon, "Lettres à la diaspora" (1921), in *Écrits, t. I La nation et le travail* (Jerusalem: Zionist Library, 1952), p. 560 (in Hebrew). Quoted in Sternhell, *Founding Myths of Israel*, pp. 71–72.

20 Sternhell, *Founding Myths of Israel*, p. 72.

21 Theodor Herzl, *The Jewish State: An Attempt at a Modern Solution of the Jewish Question*, tr. Sylvie d'Avigdor (London: Pordes, 1967).

22 The United States supplies Israel with $3.3 billion in military aid per year ($158 billion total to date). See Lara Jakes, "For Many Western Allies, Sending Weapons to Israel Gets Dicey," *The New York Times*, April 13, 2024; and Jean-Philippe Lefief, "Israël : qui sont ses principaux fournisseurs d'armes?" *Le Monde*, March 22, 2024.

3. Reason of State

1 See Susan Neiman, director of the Einstein Forum in Potsdam: "Germany on Edge," *The New York Review of Books*, Nov. 3, 2023.

2 On the republican thinker see J. G. A. Pocock, *The Machiavellian Moment: Florentine Political Thought and the*

Atlantic Republican Tradition (Princeton: Princeton University Press, 2017 [1975]); the "teacher of evil" is depicted by Leo Strauss, *Thoughts on Machiavelli* (Chicago: University of Chicago Press, 1958). For a brilliant reevaluation of Machiavelli's republicanism see Patrick Boucheron, *Machiavelli: The Art of Teaching People What to Fear*, tr. Willard Wood (New York: Other Press, 2020).

3   Norberto Bobbio, *Teoria generale della politica*, ed. Michelangelo Bovero (Turin: Einaudi, 1999), p. 119.

4   Bobbio, *Teoria generale della politica*, pp. 173–174. See Gabriel Naudé, *Considérations politiques sur les coups d'État* (1639), ed. Lionel Leforestier, Maxime Leroy, and Frédérique Main (Paris: Le Promeneur, 2004).

5   On the role played by Holocaust memory in reinforcing the political and diplomatic relationship between Germany and the United States, see Jacob S. Eder, *Holocaust Angst: The Federal Republic of Germany and American Holocaust Memory since the 1970s* (New York: Oxford University Press, 2016).

6   See Pankaj Mishra, "Memory Failure," *London Review of Books*, vol. 46, n. 1, Jan. 4, 2024. See also Esra Özyürek, *Subcontractors of Guilt: Holocaust Memory and Muslim Belonging in Postwar Germany* (Stanford: Stanford University Press, 2023).

7   Omer Bartov, *Weaponizing Language: Misuses of Holocaust Memory and the Never Again Syndrome*, Council for Global Cooperation, March 12, 2024, https://cgcinternational .co.in/weaponizing-language-misuses-of-holocaust -memory-and-the-never-again-syndrome.

8   I summarized this old debate in Enzo Traverso, "The Uniqueness of Auschwitz: Hypotheses, Problems, and Wrong Turns in Historical Research" (1997), *Critique of Modern Barbarism: Essays on Fascism, Anti-Semitism, and the Use of History*, tr. Peter Drucker (London: Resistance Books, 2018), pp. 106–128.

4. False News of the War

1 Marc Bloch, "Reflections of a Historian on the False News of the War," tr. James P. Holoka, *Michigan War Studies Review*, July 1, 2013 [1921].

2 Bloch, "Reflections of a Historian."

3 For a critical reconstruction of this debate, see Sabina Loriga, "Une vieille affaire? Les *Pâques de sang* d'Ariel Toaff," *Annales. Histoire, Sciences Sociales*, 2008, vol. 63, n. 1, pp. 143–172. See Ariel Toaff, *Pasque di sangue. Ebrei d'Europa e omicidi rituali* (Bologna: Il Mulino, 2008).

5. Anti-Zionism and Anti-Semitism

1 Isaac Deutscher, *The Non-Jewish Jew and Other Essays* (London-New York: Verso Books, 2017 [1968]).

2 See Pierre Vidal-Naquet, *Mémoires. Le trouble et la lumière 1955–1998* (Paris: Seuil/La Découverte, 1998), p. 159.

3 For a summary of the historiographic debate surrounding the Haavara Agreements, see Hava Eshkoli-Wagman, "Yishuv Zionism: Its Attitude to Nazism and the Third Reich Reconsidered," *Modern Judaism*, vol. 19, n. 1, 1999, pp. 21–40.

4 See Daniel Lindenberg: *Figures d'Israël. L'identité juive entre marranisme et sionisme (1648-1998)* (Paris: Hachette, 1997).

5 Bloch, "Reflections of a Historian."

6 For a summary of the trial, see Tzvetan Todorov, *Hope and Memory: Lessons from the Twentieth Century*, tr. David Bellos (Princeton: Princeton University Press, 2003), pp. 148–158.

7 See Enzo Traverso, *The End of Jewish Modernity*, tr. David Fernbach (London: Pluto Press, 2016), ch. 7, "The Civil Religion of the Holocaust," pp. 113–127.

8 According to Nonna Mayer, who provides a yearly status report on racism and anti-Semitism in France for the Commission nationale consultative des droits de l'homme: "Since 1990, this poll has shown that tolerance toward all

minorities has increased, although the hierarchy between them has persisted, from the Romani, who are the most discriminated against, to the Blacks and the Jews, who are the most accepted." See *Le Monde*, Nov. 10, 2023. The data is analogous for most countries of Europe and America.

6. Violence, Terrorism, Resistance

1 Benny Morris, *Righteous Victims: A History of the Zionist-Arab Conflicts, 1881–2001* (New York: Vintage Books, 2001), p. 208.

2 One of the more significant moments, in 1938, was an exchange between the anarchist writer Victor Serge, the Marxist Leon Trotsky, and the liberal philosopher John Dewey, collected in Leon Trotsky, *Their Moral and Ours*, introduction by George Novack (New York: Pathfinder Press, 1973). I have summarized their debate in Enzo Traverso, *Fire and Blood: The European Civil War 1914–1945*, tr. David Fernbach (London–New York: Verso, 2016), pp. 245–253.

3 One of the most insightful analyses of the October 7 attack and Hamas's motivations was written within days by Adam Shatz, "Vengeful Pathologies," *London Review of Books*, vol. 45, n. 20, Oct. 19, 2023.

4 Jean-Pierre Filiu, "The Twelve Wars on Gaza," *Journal of Palestinian Studies*, vol. 14, n. 1, 2014, p. 67. Filiu is the author of the best study on the topic, *Gaza: A History* (New York: Oxford University Press, 2017).

5 Bassem Naeem, "Hamas Condemns the Holocaust," *The Guardian*, May 12, 2008.

6 See Pierre Prier, "Qu'est-ce que le Hamas?" *Orient XXI*, Dec. 13, 2021.

7 Anne Applebaum, *Gulag: A History* (New York: Anchor Books, 2004), pp. 448–449.

8 The image of the besieged city was used by the American writer Upton Sinclair, who supported Stalinism during the

1930s, in his debate with Eugene Lyons. See Upton Sinclair and Eugene Lyons, *Terror in Russia? Two Views* (New York: R. R. Smith, 1938), p. 57. On anti-fascist intellectuals and Stalinism, see Traverso, *Fire and Blood*, ch. 8, esp. pp. 265–272.

9 See Carl Schmitt, *Theory of the Partisan: Intermediate Commentary on the Concept of the Political*, tr. G. L. Ulmen (New York: Telos Press, 2007 [1962]).

10 On this point, see Nicolas Tavaglione, "Les habits de la mort. Sur la différence morale entre terrorisme et guerre légale," *Raisons politiques*, n. 41, 2011, pp. 141–169.

11 Frantz Fanon, *The Wretched of the Earth*, tr. Constance Farrington (New York: Grove Press, 1965).

12 Jean Améry, *At the Mind's Limits: Contemplations by a Survivor on Auschwitz and Its Realities*, tr. Sidney Rosenfeld and Stella P. Rosenfeld (Bloomington, IN: Indiana University Press, 1980).

13 Jean Améry, "The Birth of Man from the Spirit of Violence: Frantz Fanon the Revolutionary" (1969), tr. Adrian Daub, *Wasafiri*, vol. 20, 2005, p. 16.

14 Fanon, *The Wretched of the Earth*, p. 94.

15 Quoted in Saidiya Hartman, *Lose Your Mother: A Journey Along the Atlantic Slave Revolt* (New York: Farrar, Straus and Giroux, 2007), pp. 91–92.

16 Norbert Elias, *The Civilizing Process* (London: Blackwell, 2000 [1939]).

17 Claudio Pavone. *A Civil War: A History of Italian Resistance*, tr. Stanislao Pugliese (London–New York: Verso, 2013 [1990]), p. 497.

18 Quoted in Santo Peli, *Storie di GAP. Terrorismo urbano e Resistenza* (Turin: Einaudi, 2017), p. 209.

19 Giorgio Bocca, *Storia dell'Italia partigiana* (Bari-Roma: Laterza, 1966), p. 135. Also quoted in Peli, *Storia di GAP*, p. 28.

20 On the history of the Affiche Rouge, see Philippe Robrieux, *L'Affaire Manouchian. Vie et mort d'un héro communiste*

(Paris: Fayard, 1986); and Benoît Rayski, *L'Affiche rouge* (Paris: Denoël, 2009). Forty years ago, the filmmaker Mosco Boucault made an excellent documentary on the Manouchian group, based on the accounts of several of its members who survived the war. It was called *Des terroristes à la retraite*. In the version that is available today on the channel Arte and on DVD, the title has been changed: *terroristes* has been placed in quotation marks.

21 Peli, *Storie di GAP*, p. 64.

22 See Miriam Gebhardt, *Crimes Unspoken: The Rape of German Women at the End of the Second World War*, tr. Nick Somers (Cambridge: Polity Press, 2017).

23 See Azadeh Moaveni, "What They Did to Our Women," *London Review of Books*, 46/9, May 9, 2024.

24 Adania Shibli, *Minor Detail* (2017), tr. Elisabeth Jaquette (London: Fitzcarraldo Editions, 2020).

25 In March 2019, at a Likud meeting, Benjamin Netanyahu said, "Those who want to stop the creation of a Palestinian state must support the strengthening of Hamas [...]. This is part of our strategy: to separate the Palestinians of Gaza from those of Judea and Samaria [the West Bank]." Quoted in Adam Raz, "A Brief History of the Netanyahu-Hamas Alliance," *Haaretz*, Oct. 20, 2023.

7. Crossed Memories

1 See Rashid Khalidi, *Palestinian Identity: The Construction of Modern National Consciousness* (New York: Columbia University Press, 2009), and Elias Sanbar, *Figures du Palestinien. Identité des origines, identité du devenir* (Paris: Gallimard, 2004).

2 Edward W. Said, *From Oslo to Iraq and the Road Map*, introduction by Tony Judt (New York: Pantheon Books, 2004), p. 67.

3 Fanon, *The Wretched of the Earth*, p. 42.

4 See Oliver Holmes and Ruth Michaelson, "Israel Declares Siege of Gaza as Hamas Threatens to Start Killing Hostages," *The Guardian*, Oct. 10, 2023.

5 Quoted by Tony Judt in his foreword to Edward Said's *From Oslo to Iraq*, p. xix.

6 Judy Rudoren, "Netanyahu Denounced for Saying Palestinians Inspired Holocaust," *The New York Times*, Oct. 21, 2015. On the relation of Amir Al-Hussein to Nazism, of which he was an accomplice but certainly not an inspiration, see Gilbert Achcar, *The Arabs and the Holocaust: The Arab-Israeli War of Narratives*, tr. G.M. Goshgarian (New York: Metropolitan Books, 2009), pp. 150–157.

7 Yehuda Elkana, "For Forgetting," *Haaretz*, March 16, 1988. Quoted by Tom Segev, *The Seventh Million: The Israelis and the Holocaust*, tr. Haim Watzman (New York: Hill and Wang, 1993), pp. 502–503. On the virtues of forgetfulness, see also David Rieff, *In Praise of Forgetting: Historical Memory and Its Ironies* (New Haven: Yale University Press, 2016).

8 Primo Levi, *Conversazioni e interviste 1963–1987*, ed. Marco Belpoliti (Turin: Einaudi, 1997), p. 302.

9 Levi, *Conversazioni e interviste 1963–1987*, p. 298.

10 Judt, "Foreword," in Said, *From Oslo to Iraq*, p. xx.

11 On the souvenir photos from the partisan war (*Partisanenkampf*) taken by German soldiers, see Dieter Reifahrth and Viktoria Schmidt-Linsenhoff, "Die Kamera der Täter," in Hannes Heer and Klaus Naumann, eds., *Vernichtungskrieg, Verbrechen der Wehrmacht 1941 bis 1944* (Hamburg: Hamburger Edition, 1995), pp. 475–503. On the selfies and videos taken by Israeli soldiers in Gaza, thoroughly documented by Al Jazeera and other news channels, see Sophia Goodfriend, "The Viral Atrocities Posted by Israeli Soldiers," *Sapiens: Anthropology Magazine*, March 20, 2024; and Samuel Forey, "Des soldats

israéliens déployés à Gaza mettent en scène leurs exactions sur les réseaux sociaux," *Le Monde*, Feb. 28, 2024.

8. *From the River to the Sea*

1 On the uses of this slogan, see Alon Confino and Amos Goldberg, "From the River to the Sea, There Is Space for Many Different Interpretations," *Public Seminar*, April 9, 2024.

2 See Arnold Foster and Benjamin R. Epstein, *The New Anti-Semitism* (New York: McGraw-Hill, 1974). On the genealogy of this ideological vision, see Adam Haber and Matylda Figlerowicz, "Anatomy of a Moral Panic," *Jewish Currents*, May 2, 2024.

3 See Sylvain Cypel, *The State of Israel vs. the Jews*, pp. 98–101.

4 See Friedrich Ratzel, *Der Lebensraum. Eine biogeographische Studie* (Darmstadt: Wissenschaftliche Buchgesellschaft, 1966 [1901]); for a critical study of the development of this concept, see Diner, *Beyond the Conceivable*, ch. 2, "Knowledge of Expansion: On the Geopolitics of Karl Haushofer," pp. 26–48.

5 Amnon Raz-Krakotzkin, *Exil et souveraineté. Judaisme, sionisme et pensée binationale*, foreword by Carlo Ginzburg (Paris: La fabrique, 2007), p. 210.

6 Hannah Arendt and Gershom Scholem, *Der Briefwechsel 1939-1964* (Berlin: Jüdischer Verlag, 2010), pp. 110, 133–134. On the history of Zionism and its different components, see Walter Laqueur, *History of Zionism* (New York: Schocken Books, 1976 [1972]). On cultural Zionism and binationalism, see Raz-Krakotzkin, *Exil et souveraineté*.

7 See Walter Laqueur, *History of Zionism*, and the very rich anthology edited and introduced by Denis Charbit, *Sionismes. Textes fondamentaux* (Paris: Albin Michel, 1998). Charbit quite correctly uses the plural "Zionisms" in his title.

8 Hannah Arendt, "Peace or Armistice in the Near East?" in *The Jewish Writings*, p. 444.

9 Arendt, "To Save the Jewish Homeland," in *The Jewish Writings*, pp. 396–397.

10 Arendt, "Peace or Armistice," in *The Jewish Writings*, p. 441.

11 Said, *From Oslo to Iraq*, p. 197.

12 Quoted in Tom Segev, *The Seventh Million: The Israelis and the Holocaust*, tr. Haim Watzman (New York: Hill and Wang, 1993).

13 See Lucas Minisini, "Qui est le journaliste israélien Yuval Abraham, qui a plaidé pour un cessez-le-feu à Gaza," *Le Monde*, March 6, 2024. Several German politicians called Abraham's speech anti-Semitic.

14 "Mai indifferenti. Voci ebraiche per la pace," *Il Fatto Quotidiano*, Feb. 11, 2024.

15 "Nous, Françaises juives et Français juifs, appelons à un cessez-le-feu immédiat et durable à Gaza," *Le Monde*, Jan. 30, 2024.

About the Author

Enzo Traverso was born in Italy and taught history and political theory in France for almost twenty years. Since 2013, he teaches at Cornell University. He is the author of several books, including *The End of Jewish Modernity, Fire and Blood: The European Civil War, Left-Wing Melancholia, The New Faces of Fascism, Singular Pasts: The "I" in Historiography*, and *Revolution: An Intellectual History*, which have been translated into many languages. He regularly writes for *Jacobin* in the United States, *Il Manifesto* in Italy, and French and Spanish-language magazines. He has also taught as visiting professor in several countries across Europe and Latin America.

About the Translator

Willard Wood grew up in France and has translated more than thirty works of fiction and nonfiction from the French. He has won the Lewis Galantière Award for Literary Translation and received a National Endowment for the Arts Fellowship in Translation. He lives in Norfolk, Connecticut.